Securing Hadoop

Implement robust end-to-end security for your Hadoop ecosystem

Sudheesh Narayanan

BIRMINGHAM - MUMBAI

Securing Hadoop

First published: November 2013

Production Reference: 1181113

Published by Packt Publishing Ltd.
Livery Place
35 Livery Street
Birmingham B3 2PB, UK.

ISBN 978-1-78328-525-9

www.packtpub.com

Cover Image by Ravaji Babu (ravaji_babu@outlook.com)

Credits

Author
Sudheesh Narayanan

Reviewers
Mark Kerzner

Nitin Pawar

Acquisition Editor
Antony Lowe

Commissioning Editor
Shaon Basu

Technical Editors
Amit Ramadas

Amit Shetty

Project Coordinator
Akash Poojary

Proofreader
Ameesha Green

Indexer
Rekha Nair

Graphics
Sheetal Aute

Ronak Dhruv

Valentina D'silva

Disha Haria

Abhinash Sahu

Production Coordinator
Nilesh R. Mohite

Cover Work
Nilesh R. Mohite

About the Author

Sudheesh Narayanan is a Technology Strategist and Big Data Practitioner with expertise in technology consulting and implementing Big Data solutions. With over 15 years of IT experience in Information Management, Business Intelligence, Big Data & Analytics, and Cloud & J2EE application development, he provided his expertise in architecting, designing, and developing Big Data products, Cloud management platforms, and highly scalable platform services. His expertise in Big Data includes Hadoop and its ecosystem components, NoSQL databases (MongoDB, Cassandra, and HBase), Text Analytics (GATE and OpenNLP), Machine Learning (Mahout, Weka, and R), and Complex Event Processing.

Sudheesh is currently working with Genpact as the Assistant Vice President and Chief Architect – Big Data, with focus on driving innovation and building Intellectual Property assets, frameworks, and solutions. Prior to Genpact, he was the co-inventor and Chief Architect of the Infosys BigDataEdge product.

I would like to thank my wife, Smita and son, Aryan for their sacrifices and support during this journey, and my dad, mom, and sister for encouraging me at all times to make a difference by contributing back to the community. This book would not have been possible without their encouragement and constant support.

Special thanks to Rupak and Debika for investing their personal time over weekends to help me experiment with a few ideas on Hadoop security, and for being the bouncing board.

I would like to thank Shwetha, Sivaram, Ajay, Manpreet, and Venky for providing constant feedback and helping me make continuous improvements in my securing Hadoop journey.

Above all, I would like to acknowledge my sincere thanks to my teacher, Prof. N. C. Jain; my leaders and coach Paddy, Vishnu Bhat, Sandeep Bhagat, Jaikrishnan, Anil D'Souza, and KNM Rao for their mentoring and guidance in making me who I am today, so that I could write this book.

About the Reviewers

Mark Kerzner holds degrees in Law, Math, and Computer Science. He has been designing software for many years and Hadoop-based systems since 2008. He is the President of SHMsoft, a provider of Hadoop applications for various verticals, and a co-author of the Hadoop illuminated book/project. He has authored and co-authored books and patents.

> I would like to acknowledge the help of my colleagues, in particular, Sujee Maniyam, and last but not the least, my multitalented family.

Nitin Pawar started his career as a Release Engineer and Tools Developer, then moved into different roles such as operations, solutions engineering, process engineering, and Big Data analytics. Currently, he is working as a Big Data System Architect, and trying to solve problems related to customer success management. He has mainly been working with technologies revolving around the first generation Hadoop ecosystem.

www.PacktPub.com

Support files, eBooks, discount offers and more

You might want to visit www.PacktPub.com for support files and downloads related to your book.

Did you know that Packt offers eBook versions of every book published, with PDF and ePub files available? You can upgrade to the eBook version at www.PacktPub.com and as a print book customer, you are entitled to a discount on the eBook copy. Get in touch with us at service@packtpub.com for more details.

At www.PacktPub.com, you can also read a collection of free technical articles, sign up for a range of free newsletters and receive exclusive discounts and offers on Packt books and eBooks.

http://PacktLib.PacktPub.com

Do you need instant solutions to your IT questions? PacktLib is Packt's online digital book library. Here, you can access, read and search across Packt's entire library of books.

Why Subscribe?

- Fully searchable across every book published by Packt
- Copy and paste, print and bookmark content
- On demand and accessible via web browser

Free Access for Packt account holders

If you have an account with Packt at www.PacktPub.com, you can use this to access PacktLib today and view nine entirely free books. Simply use your login credentials for immediate access.

Table of Contents

Preface

Today, many organizations are implementing Hadoop in production environments. As organizations embark on the Big Data implementation journey, security of Big Data is one of the major concerns. Securing sensitive data is one of the top priorities for organizations. Enterprise security teams are worried about integrating Hadoop security with enterprise systems. *Securing Hadoop* provides a detailed implementation and best practices for securing a Hadoop-based Big Data platform. It covers the fundamentals behind Kerberos security and Hadoop security design, and then details the approach for securing Hadoop and its ecosystem components within an enterprise context. The goal of this book is to take an end-to-end enterprise view on Big Data security by looking at the Big Data security reference architecture, and detailing how the various building blocks required by an organization can be put together to establish a secure Big Data platform.

What this book covers

Chapter 1, Hadoop Security Overview, highlights the key challenges and requirements that should be considered for securing any Hadoop-based Big Data platform. We then provide an enterprise view of Big Data security and detail the Big Data security reference architecture.

Chapter 2, Hadoop Security Design, details the internals of the Hadoop security design and explains the key concepts required for understanding and implementing Kerberos security. The focus of this chapter is to arrive at a common understanding of various terminologies and concepts required for remainder of this book.

Chapter 3, Setting Up a Secured Hadoop Cluster, provides a step-by-step guide on configuring Kerberos and establishing a secured Hadoop cluster.

Chapter 4, Securing the Hadoop Ecosystem, looks at the detailed internal interaction and communication protocols for each of the Hadoop ecosystem components along with the security gaps. We then provide a step-by-step guide to establish a secured Big Data ecosystem.

Chapter 5, Integrating Hadoop with Enterprise Security Systems, focuses on the implementation approach to integrate Hadoop security models with enterprise security systems and how to centrally manage access controls for users in a secured Hadoop platform.

Chapter 6, Securing Sensitive Data in Hadoop, provides a detailed implementation approach for securing sensitive data within a Hadoop ecosystem and what are the various data encryption techniques used in securing Big Data platforms.

Chapter 7, Security Event and Audit Logging in Hadoop, provides a deep dive into the security incident and event monitoring system that needs to be implemented in a secured Big Data platform. We then provide the best practices and approach for implementing these security procedures and policies.

Appendix, Solutions Available for Securing Hadoop, provides an overview of the various commercial and open source technologies that are available to build a secured Hadoop Big Data ecosystem. We look into details of each of these technologies and where they fit into the overall Big Data security reference architecture.

What you need for this book

To practice the examples provided in this book, you will need a working Hadoop cluster. You will also need a multinode Linux cluster (a minimum of 2 nodes of CentOS 6.2 or similar). Cloudera CDH4.1 or above is recommended. Any latest version of Apache Hadoop distribution can also be used instead of CDH4.1.You will have to download and install Kerberos 5 Release 1.11.3 from the MIT site (http://web.mit.edu/kerberos/krb5-1.11/).

Who this book is for

Securing Hadoop is ideal for Hadoop practitioners (Big Data architects, developers, and administrators) who have some working knowledge of Hadoop and wants to implement security for Hadoop. This book is also for Big Data architects who want to design and implement an end-to-end secured Big Data solution for an enterprise context. This book will also act as reference guide for the administrators who are on the implementation and configuration of Hadoop security.

Conventions

In this book, you will find a number of styles of text that distinguish between different kinds of information. Here are some examples of these styles, and an explanation of their meaning.

Code words in text are shown as follows: "To support renewable tickets, we add the `max_renewable_life` setting to your realm in `kdc.conf`."

A block of code is set as follows:

```
kdcdefaults]
kdc_ports = 88

[realms]
MYDOMAIN.COM = {
  profile = /etc/krb5.conf
  supported_enctypes = aes128-cts:normal des3-hmac-sha1:normal
    arcfour-hmac:normal des-hmac-sha1:normal des-cbc-md5:normal des-
      cbc-crc:normal des-cbc-crc:v4 des-cbc-crc:afs3
  allow-null-ticket-addresses = true
  database_name = /usr/local/var/krb5kdc/principal
  acl_file = /usr/local/var/krb5kdc/kadm5.acl
  admin_database_lockfile = /usr/local/var/krb5kd/kadm5_adb.lock
  admin_keytab = FILE:/usr/local/var/krb5kdc/kadm5.keytab
  key_stash_file = /usr/local/var/krb5kdc/.k5stash
  kdc_ports = 88
  kadmind_port = 749
  max_life = 2d 0h 0m 0s
  max_renewable_life = 7d 0h 0m 0s
}
```

Any command-line input or output is written as follows:

```
sudo service hadoop-hdfs-namenode start
sudo service hadoop-hdfs-datanode start
sudo service hadoop-hdfs-secondarynamenode start
For MRV1
sudo service hadoop-0.20-mapreduce-jobtracker start
```

New terms and **important words** are shown in bold. Words that you see on the screen, in menus or dialog boxes for example, appear in the text like this: "clicking the **Next** button moves you to the next screen".

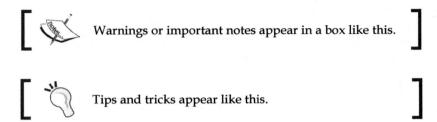

Warnings or important notes appear in a box like this.

Tips and tricks appear like this.

Reader feedback

Feedback from our readers is always welcome. Let us know what you think about this book—what you liked or may have disliked. Reader feedback is important for us to develop titles that you really get the most out of.

To send us general feedback, simply send an e-mail to feedback@packtpub.com, and mention the book title via the subject of your message.

If there is a topic that you have expertise in and you are interested in either writing or contributing to a book, see our author guide on www.packtpub.com/authors.

Customer support

Now that you are the proud owner of a Packt book, we have a number of things to help you to get the most from your purchase.

Errata

Although we have taken every care to ensure the accuracy of our content, mistakes do happen. If you find a mistake in one of our books—maybe a mistake in the text or the code—we would be grateful if you would report this to us. By doing so, you can save other readers from frustration and help us improve subsequent versions of this book. If you find any errata, please report them by visiting http://www.packtpub.com/submit-errata, selecting your book, clicking on the **errata submission form** link, and entering the details of your errata. Once your errata are verified, your submission will be accepted and the errata will be uploaded on our website, or added to any list of existing errata, under the Errata section of that title. Any existing errata can be viewed by selecting your title from http://www.packtpub.com/support.

Piracy

Piracy of copyright material on the Internet is an ongoing problem across all media. At Packt, we take the protection of our copyright and licenses very seriously. If you come across any illegal copies of our works, in any form, on the Internet, please provide us with the location address or website name immediately so that we can pursue a remedy.

Please contact us at copyright@packtpub.com with a link to the suspected pirated material.

We appreciate your help in protecting our authors, and our ability to bring you valuable content.

Questions

You can contact us at questions@packtpub.com if you are having a problem with any aspect of the book, and we will do our best to address it.

Hadoop Security Overview

Like any development project, the ones in Hadoop start with **proof of concept (POC)**. Especially because the technology is new and continuously evolving, the focus always begins with figuring out what it can offer and how to leverage it to solve different business problems, be it consumer analysis, breaking news processing, and so on. Being an open source framework, it has its own nuances and requires a learning curve. As these POCs mature and move to pilot and then to production phase, a new infrastructure has to be set up. Then questions arise around maintaining the newly setup infrastructure, including questions on data security and the overall ecosystem's security. Few of the questions that the infrastructure administrators and security paranoids would ask are:

How secure is a Hadoop ecosystem? How secure is the data residing in Hadoop? How would different teams including business analysts, data scientists, developers, and others in the enterprise access the Hadoop ecosystem in a secure manner? How to enforce existing **Enterprise Security Models** in this new infrastructure? Are there any best practices for securing such an infrastructure?

This chapter will begin the journey to answer these questions and provide an overview of the typical challenges faced in securing Hadoop-based **Big Data** ecosystem. We will look at the key security considerations and then present the security reference architecture that can be used for securing Hadoop.

The following topics will be covered in this chapter:

- Why do we need to secure a Hadoop-based ecosystem?
- The challenges in securing such an infrastructure
- Important security considerations for a Hadoop ecosystem
- The reference architecture for securing a Hadoop ecosystem

Why do we need to secure Hadoop?

Enterprise data consists of crucial information related to sales, customer interactions, human resources, and so on, and is locked securely within systems such as ERP, CRM, and general ledger systems. In the last decade, enterprise data security has matured significantly as organizations learned their lessons from various data security incidents that caused them losses in billions. As the services industry has grown and matured, most of the systems are outsourced to vendors who deal with crucial client information most of the time. As a result, security and privacy standards such as HIPAA, HITECH, PCI, SOX, ISO, and COBIT have evolved . This requires service providers to comply with these regulatory standards to fully safeguard their client's data assets. This has resulted in a very protective data security enforcement within enterprises including service providers as well as the clients. There is absolutely no tolerance to data security violations. Over the last eight years of its development, Hadoop has now reached a mature state where enterprises have started adopting it for their Big Data processing needs. The prime use case is to gain strategic and operational advantages from their humongous data sets. However, to do any analysis on top of these datasets, we need to bring them to the Hadoop ecosystem for processing. So the immediate question that arises with respect to data security is, how secure is the data storage inside the Hadoop ecosystem?

The question is not just about securing the source data which is moved from the enterprise systems to the Hadoop ecosystem. Once these datasets land into the Hadoop ecosystems, analysts and data scientists perform large-scale analytics and machine-learning-based processing to derive business insights. These business insights are of great importance to the enterprise. Any such insights in the hands of the competitor or any unauthorized personnel could be disastrous to the business. It is these business insights that are highly sensitive and must be fully secured.

Any data security incident will cause business users to lose their trust in the ecosystem. Unless the business teams have confidence in the Hadoop ecosystem, they won't take the risk to invest in Big Data. Hence, the success and failure of Big Data-related projects really depends upon how secure our data ecosystem is going to be.

Challenges for securing the Hadoop ecosystem

Big Data not only brings challenges for storing, processing, and analysis but also for managing and securing these large data assets. Hadoop was not built with security to begin with. As enterprises started adopting Hadoop, the Kerberos-based security model evolved within Hadoop. But given the distributed nature of the ecosystem and wide range of applications that are built on top of Hadoop, securing Hadoop from an enterprise context is a big challenge.

A typical Big Data ecosystem has multiple stakeholders who interact with the system. For example, expert users (business analysts and data scientists) within the organization would interact with the ecosystem using **business intelligence (BI)** and analytical tools, and would need deep data access to the data to perform various analysis. A finance department business analyst should not be able to see the data from the HR department and so on. BI tools need a wide range of system-level access to the Hadoop ecosystem depending on the protocol and data that they use for communicating with the ecosystem.

One of the biggest challenges for Big Data projects within enterprises today is about securely integrating the external data sources (social blogs, websites, existing ERP and CRM systems, and so on). This external connectivity needs to be established so that the extracted data from these external sources is available in the Hadoop ecosystem.

Hadoop ecosystem tools such as **Sqoop** and **Flume** were not built with full enterprise grade security. Cloudera, MapR, and few others have made significant contributions towards enabling these ecosystem components to be enterprise grade, resulting in **Sqoop 2**, **Flume-ng**, and **Hive Server 2**. Apart from these, there are multiple security-focused projects within the Hadoop ecosystem such as **Cloudera Sentry** (http://www.cloudera.com/content/cloudera/en/products/cdh/sentry.html), **Hortonworks Knox Gateway** (http://hortonworks.com/hadoop/knox-gateway/), and Intel's **Project Rhino** (https://github.com/intel-hadoop/project-rhino/). These projects are making significant progress to make Apache Hadoop provide enterprise grade security. A detailed understanding of each of these ecosystem components is needed to deploy them in production.

Another area of concern within enterprises is the need the existing enterprise **Identity and Access Management (IDAM)** systems with the Hadoop ecosystem. With such integration, enterprises can extend the Identity and Access Management to the Hadoop ecosystem. However, these integrations bring in multiple challenges as Hadoop inherently has not been built with such enterprise integrations in mind.

Apart from ecosystem integration, there is often a need to have sensitive information within the Big Data ecosystem, to derive patterns and inferences from these datasets. As we move these datasets to the Big Data ecosystem we need to mask/encrypt this sensitive information. Traditional data masking and encryption tools don't scale well for large scale Big Data masking and encryption. We need to identify new means for encryption of large scale datasets.

Usually, as the adoption of Big Data increases, enterprises quickly move to a multicluster/multiversion scenario, where there are multiple versions of the Hadoop ecosystem operating in an enterprise. Also, sensitive data that was earlier banned from the Big Data platform slowly makes its way in. This brings in additional challenges on how we address security in such a complex environment, as a small lapse in security could result in huge financial loss for the organization.

Key security considerations

As discussed previously, to meet the enterprise data security needs for a Big Data ecosystem, a complex and holistic approach is needed to secure the entire ecosystem. Some of the key security considerations while securing Hadoop-based Big Data ecosystem are:

- **Authentication**: There is a need to provide a single point for authentication that is aligned and integrated with existing enterprise identity and access management system.

- **Authorization**: We need to enforce a role-based authorization with fine-grained access control for providing access to sensitive data.

- **Access control**: There is a need to control who can do what on a dataset, and who can use how much of the processing capacity available in the cluster.

- **Data masking and encryption**: We need to deploy proper encryption and masking techniques on data to ensure secure access to sensitive data for authorized personnel.

- **Network perimeter security**: We need to deploy perimeter security for the overall Hadoop ecosystem that controls how the data can move in and move out of the ecosystem to other infrastructures. Design and implement the network topology to provide proper isolation of the Big Data ecosystem from the rest of the enterprise. Provide proper network-level security by configuring the appropriate firewall rules to prevent unauthorized traffic.

- **System security**: There is a need to provide system-level security by hardening the OS and the applications that are installed as part of the ecosystem. Address all the known vulnerability of OS and applications.

- **Infrastructure security**: We need to enforce strict infrastructure and physical access security in the data center.

- **Audits and event monitoring**: A proper audit trial is required for any changes to the data ecosystem and provide audit reports for various activities (data access and data processing) that occur within the ecosystem.

Reference architecture for Big Data security

Implementing all the preceding security considerations for the enterprise data security becomes very vital to building a trusted Big Data ecosystem within the enterprise. The following figure shows as a typical Big Data ecosystem and how various ecosystem components and stakeholders interact with each other. Implementing the security controls in each of these interactions requires elaborate planning and careful execution.

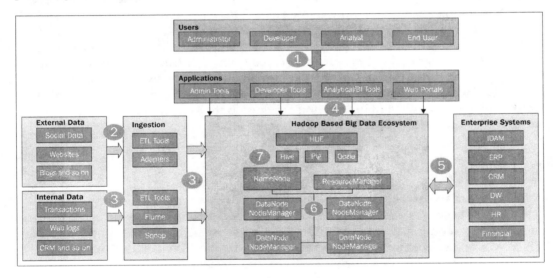

The reference architecture depicted in the following diagram summarizes the key security pillars that needs to be considered for securing a Big Data ecosystem. In the next chapters, we will explore how to leverage the Hadoop security model and the various existing enterprise tools to secure the Big Data ecosystem.

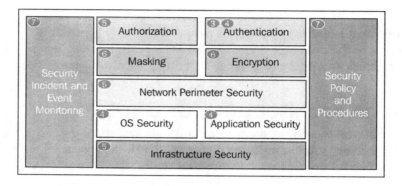

In *Chapter 4, Securing the Hadoop Ecosystem*, we will look at the implementation details to secure the OS and applications that are deployed along with Hadoop in the ecosystem. In *Chapter 5, Integrating Hadoop with Enterprise Security Systems*, we look at the corporate network perimeter security requirement and how to secure the cluster and look at how authorization defined within the enterprise identity management system can be integrated with the Hadoop ecosystem. In *Chapter 6, Securing Sensitive Data in Hadoop*, we look at the encryption implementation for securing sensitive data in Hadoop. In *Chapter 7, Security Event and Audit Logging in Hadoop*, we look at security incidents and event monitoring along with the security policies required to address the audit and reporting requirements.

Summary

In this chapter, we understood the overall security challenges for securing Hadoop-based Big Data ecosystem deployments. We looked at the two different types (source and insights) of data that is stored in the Hadoop ecosystem and how important it is to secure these datasets to retain business confidence. We detailed out the key security considerations for securing Hadoop, and presented the overall security reference architecture that can be used as a guiding light for the overall security design of a Big Data ecosystem. In the rest of the book, we will use this reference architecture as a guide to implement the Hadoop-based secured Big Data ecosystem.

In the next chapter, we will look in depth at the Kerberos security model and how this is deployed in a secured Hadoop cluster. We will look at the Hadoop security model in detail and understand the key design considerations based on the current Hadoop security implementation.

2
Hadoop Security Design

In *Chapter 1, Hadoop Security Overview*, we discussed the security considerations for an end-to-end Hadoop-based Big Data ecosystem. In this chapter, we will narrow our focus and take a deep dive into the security design of the Hadoop platform. Hadoop security was implemented as part of the HADOOP-4487 Jira issue, starting in late 2009 (`https://issues.apache.org/jira/browse/HADOOP-4487`). Currently, there are efforts to implement SSO Authentication in Hadoop. This is currently not production-ready, and hence will be out of scope of this book.

Hadoop security implementation is based on Kerberos. So in this chapter, first we will be provided with a high-level overview of key Kerberos terminologies and concepts, and then we will look into the details of the Hadoop security implementation.

The following are the topics we'll be covering in this chapter:

- What is Kerberos?
- The Hadoop default security model
- The Hadoop Kerberos security implementation

What is Kerberos?

In any distributed system, when two parties (the client and server) have to communicate over the network, the first step in this communication is to establish trust between these parties. This is usually done through the authentication process, where the client presents its password to the server and the server verifies this password. If the client sends passwords over an unsecured network, there is a risk of passwords getting compromised as they travel through the network.

Kerberos is a secured network authentication protocol that provides strong authentication for client/server applications without transferring the password over the network. Kerberos works by using time-sensitive tickets that are generated using the symmetric key cryptography. Kerberos is derived from the Greek mythology where Kerberos was the three-headed dog that guarded the gates of Hades. The three heads of Kerberos in the security paradigm are:

- The user who is trying to authenticate.
- The service to which the client is trying to authenticate.
- Kerberos security server known as **Key Distribution Center** (KDC), which is trusted by both the user and the service. The KDC stores the secret keys (passwords) for the users and services that would like to communicate with each other.

Key Kerberos terminologies

KDC provides two main functionalities known as **Authentication Service (AS)** and **Ticket Granting Service (TGS)**. AS is responsible for authenticating the users and services, while the TGS provides a ticket that is a time-limited cryptographic message. This ticket is used by the client to authenticate with the server.

The parties involved in the communication (the client and server) are known as **principals**. Each party has a principal that is defined within KDC. Each party shares the secret key (password) with the KDC. The passwords can be stored locally within KDC, but it is good practice to manage this centrally using LDAP.

Each KDC is associated with a group known as a **realm**. A realm is equivalent to a domain in Windows terminology. Principals defined within a single KDC are in the same realm. There could be multiple KDCs, and hence multiple realms in the network.

In a multiple realm scenario, a client that authenticates with one realm can connect to the server defined in another realm, as long as there is trust established between the two realms/KDCs.

KDC consists of two main daemons. These daemons are:

- **krb5kdc**: This is the Kerberos Authentication Server and is responsible for authenticating the client and also granting tickets.
- **kadmind**: This is the administrative server daemon and is responsible for performing administrative operations such as adding a new principal, changing passwords, and such other activities on KDC.

Kerberos also provides multiple utilities that are useful for working with KDC. The important utilities are:

- `kadmin` and `kadmin.local`: These are administrative clients for the **kadmind** daemon to perform administrative tasks. `kadmin.local` directly connects to the KDC database on the local server, while the `kadmin` process allows for remote connectivity.
- `kinit`: This utility is used to authenticate with the KDC and fetch the Kerberos ticket for the user.
- `klist`: This utility is used to list the Kerberos tickets currently in the client's local credential cache.
- `ktutil`: This is the key tab file utility that is used to update and view the key tab file.
- `kdb5_util`: This is the KDC database utility. This is used to create the KDC database and maintain it.

How Kerberos works?

The detailed authentication and authorization flow in a Kerberos cluster is shown in the following figure:

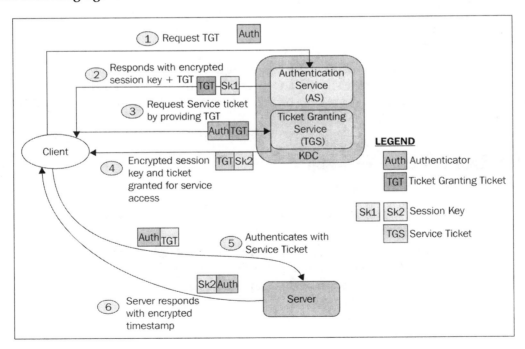

The following are the key steps involved in this flow:

1. The client sends the authentication request to KDC and requests for the **Ticket Granting Ticket (TGT).**

2. The KDC provides the TGT and session key to the client. The TGT is a special ticket provided by KDC to authenticated users, which can be used to fetch service tickets for any servers. TGT has a lifespan of 8 to 10 hours, during which the user can request for tickets for any server with which the user wants to communicate. The session key is a common key for the two parties in communication. The session key is used for encryption of data between the two parties.

3. Using the TGT, the client requests for the service ticket.

4. The KDC provides the service ticket (TGS) and the session key that can be used for encrypting data sent to the requested server. The session key is encrypted using the server's secret key, so that only the server can decrypt the session key using its secret key and communicate with the user. The session key expires after the defined time period. Usually, the time period is limited to 8 to 10 hours.

5. The client now contacts the target server and provides the TGS. The server will decrypt the TGS using the server's secret key and authenticate the client.

6. The server will provide the authenticator encrypted with the session key. Now the client and server share the session key as the secret key, which will be used for any data encryption needs.

Since the protocol is time-sensitive, it is required that all the machines which communicate with each other should have the time synchronized with a maximum lag of five minutes. If any server time offset is more than five minutes, it will not be able to authenticate.

Kerberos advantages

The key advantages of using Kerberos are:

- A password never travels over the network. Only time-sensitive tickets travel over the network.

- Passwords or secret keys are only known to the KDC and the principal. This makes the system scalable for authenticating a large number of entities, as the entities only need to know their own secret keys and set that secret key in KDC.

- Kerberos supports passwords or secret keys to be stored in a centralized credential store that is LDAP-complaint. This makes it easy for the administrators to manage the system and the users.

- Servers don't have to store any tickets or any client-specific details to authenticate a client. The authentication request will have all the required data to authenticate the client. The server only needs to know its own secret key to authenticate any client.

- The client authenticates with KDC and gets the TGT that is used for all subsequent authentications. This makes the overall authentication system faster, as there is no need for any lookup against the credential store after the first authentication is done.

The Hadoop default security model without Kerberos

Now that we understand how the Kerberos security protocol works, let us look at the details of the Hadoop default security model and its limitations.

Hadoop implements a security model similar to the POSIX filesystem, which gives the ability to apply file permissions and restrict read-write access to files and directories in HDFS. The user and admin can use the chmod and chown commands to change the permissions and ownership of the file/directories, similar to the POSIX filesystem. Hadoop does not provide any user management functionality. It uses the operating system user within Hadoop.

By default, Hadoop doesn't support any authentication of users or Hadoop services. A user only authenticates with the operating system during the logon process. After that, when the user invokes the Hadoop command, the user ID and group is set by executing whoami and bash -c groups respectively. So if a user writes their own whoami script and adds it to the path before the Linux whoami is called, the user should be able to impersonate any user including the super user in the Hadoop filesystem. The permission checks in Hadoop can be enabled by setting the property dfs.permissions to true in the hdfs-site.xml file in the configuration directory.

The following figure shows the core services and the data blocks in any Hadoop deployment:

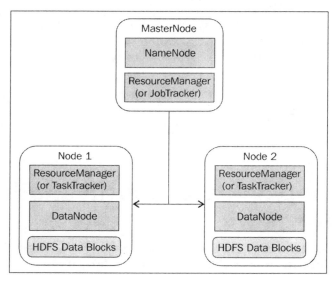

Hadoop services and data blocks

The data inside the Hadoop HDFS filesystem is stored in blocks in the **DataNode** directory. Once a user logs in to DataNodes, they can access the data blocks stored in DataNodes, based on the privilege to access the DataNode directory locally on that node. Thus, the data blocks stored in DataNode are not secured.

By default, Hadoop doesn't authenticate the services, and hence a user can run custom services on any of the machines, and this machine can be registered as DataNode or TaskTracker/NodeManager. Hadoop will replicate the data to all the Hadoop DataNodes, and hence the malicious user machine that registers with NameNode will automatically start receiving the data blocks from the Hadoop cluster. Hadoop has a setting that restricts the machines which can register as DataNodes to NameNode. If the `dfs.hosts` property in `hdfs-site.xml` points to a file that contains one host per line, only those hosts will be allowed to connect with NameNode and register. By default, this setting is turned off. This brings up a security hole where any Hadoop client can connect to any DataNode and add malicious data blocks or read any data block using the block ID.

Hadoop Kerberos security implementation

Enforcing security within a distributed system such as Hadoop is complex. The detailed requirements for securing Hadoop were identified by Owen O'Malley and others as part of the Hadoop security design. The detailed document is attached with the ticket HADOOP-4487 at `https://issues.apache.org/jira/browse/HADOOP-4487`. A summary of these requirements is explained in this section.

User-level access controls

A brief on the user-level access controls is:

- Users of Hadoop should only be able to access data that is authorized for them
- Only authenticated users should be able to submit jobs to the Hadoop cluster
- Users should be able to view, modify, and kill only their own jobs
- Only authenticated services should be able to register themselves as DataNodes or TaskTracker
- Data block access within DataNode needs to be secured, and only authenticated users should be able to access the data stored in the Hadoop cluster

Service-level access controls

Here's a gist of the service-level access controls:

- **Scalable Authentication**: Hadoop clusters consist of a large number of nodes, and the authentication models should be scalable to support such large network authentication
- **Impersonation**: Hadoop services should be able to impersonate the user submitting the job so that the correct user isolation can be maintained
- **Self-Served**: Hadoop jobs run for long durations, so they should be able to ensure that the jobs are able to self-renew the delegated user authentication to complete the job
- **Secure IPC**: Hadoop services should be able to authenticate each other and ensure secured communication between themselves

To achieve the preceding requirements, Hadoop leverages the Kerberos authentication protocol and some internal-generated tokens to secure the Hadoop cluster. Let us look into the detail of this security implementation in Hadoop.

User and service authentication

User authentication to NameNode and JobTracker services is through Hadoop's remote procedure call using the **Simple Authentication and Security Layer (SASL)** framework. Kerberos is used as the authentication protocol to authenticate the users within SASL. All Hadoop services support Kerberos authentication. A client submits the MapReduce job to JobTracker. MapReduce jobs are usually long-running jobs and they need to access the Hadoop resources on behalf of the user. This is achieved using the Delegation Token, Job Token, and the Block Access Token.

Delegation Token

A **Delegation Token** authentication is a two-party authentication protocol based on JAVA SASL Digest-MD5. A Delegation Token is used between the user and NameNode to authenticate the user. Once the user authenticates themselves with NameNode using Kerberos, the user is provided with the Delegation Token by NameNode. The user doesn't have to perform Kerberos authentication once he/ she obtains the Delegation Token. The user also designates the JobTracker or ResourceManager process as the user that will renew the Delegation Token as part of the Delegation Token request.

The Delegation Token is secured and shared with JobTracker or ResourceManager after authentication, and JobTracker will use the Delegation Token for accessing the HDFS resources on behalf of the user. JobTracker will automatically renew this Delegation Token for long-running jobs.

Job Token

A job runs on the TaskNodes and the user access has to be secured in TaskNodes. When the user submits MapReduce job to JobTracker, it will create a secret key that will be shared with TaskTracker that will run the MapReduce job. This secret key is the Job Token. The **Job Token** will be stored in the local disk of TaskTracker with permission only for the user who submitted the job. TaskTracker starts the child JVM task (mapper or reducer) using the user ID that submitted the job. Thus, the child JVM run will be able to access the Job Token from the local directory and communicate securely with TaskTracker using this Job Token. Thus, the Job Token is used to ensure that an authenticated user submitting the job in Hadoop has access to only the folders and jobs for which he is authorized in the local filesystem of TaskNodes.

Once the Reduce jobs are started in TaskTracker, this TaskTracker contacts TaskTracker that ran the Map task and fetches the mapper output files. The Job Token is also used by TaskTrackers to securely communicate with each other.

Block Access Token

Any Hadoop client requesting for data from HDFS needs to fetch the data blocks directly from DataNode after it fetches the block ID from NameNode. There should be a secured mechanism where the user privileges are securely passed to DataNode. The main purpose of the **Block Access Token** is to ensure that only authorized users are able to access the data blocks stored in DataNodes. When a client wants to access the data stored in HDFS, it requests NameNode to provide the block IDs for the files. NameNode verifies the requested user's permissions for the file and provides the list of block IDs and DataNode locations. The client then contacts DataNode to fetch the required data block. To ensure that the authentication performed by NameNode is also enforced at DataNode, Hadoop implements the BAT. BAT is the token provided by NameNode to a Hadoop client to pass data access authentication information to DataNode.

The Block Access Token implements a symmetric key encryption where both NameNode and DataNode share a common secret key. DataNode receives this secret key once it registers with NameNode and is regenerated periodically. Each of these secret keys is identified by keyID.

BAT is lightweight and contains expirationDate, keyID, ownerID, blockID, and accessModes. The access Mode defines the permission available to the user for the requested block ID. The BAT generated by NameNode is not renewable and needs to be fetched again once the token expires. BAT has a lifetime of 10 hours.

Thus, BAT ensures that the data blocks in DataNode are secured, and only authorized users can access the data blocks.

The following figure shows the various interactions in a secured Hadoop cluster:

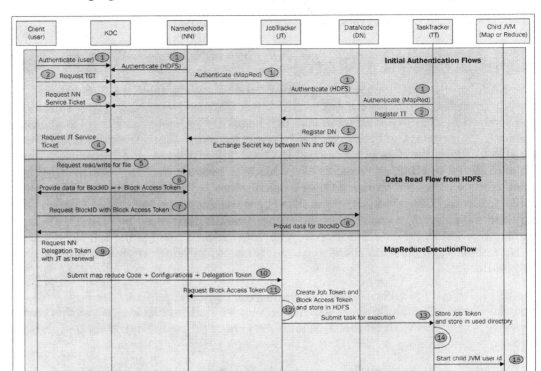

Interactions in a secured Hadoop cluster

The key steps in the overall Hadoop Kerberos operations are:

- All Hadoop services authenticate themselves with KDC. DataNode registers with NameNode. Similarly, TaskTracker registers itself with JobTracker. NodeManagers register themselves with ResourceManager.

- A client authenticates with KDC. A client requests service tickets for NameNode and JobTracker/ResourceManager.

- For any HDFS file access, a client contacts the NameNode server and requests the file. NameNode authenticates the client and provides the authorization details to the client along with the Block Access Token (BAT). The BAT is a user required by DataNode to validate the authorization of the client and provide access to corresponding blocks.

- For a MapReduce job submission in the Hadoop cluster, the client requests for a Delegation Token from JobTracker. This Delegation Token is used for submitting a MapReduce job to the cluster. The Delegation Token is renewed by JobTracker for long-running jobs.

Summary

In this chapter, we looked at the Kerberos authentication protocol and understood the key concepts involved in implementing Kerberos. We understood the default security implementation in Hadoop and how a Hadoop process gets the logged in user and group details. The default security implementation has many gaps and can't be used in production.

In a production scenario, securing Hadoop with Kerberos is essential. So we looked at the requirements that Hadoop supports at the user and Hadoop service level to secure the Hadoop cluster. We looked at the various internal secret keys (Delegation Token, Block Access Token, and Job Token) that are exchanged by the various Hadoop processes to ensure a secured ecosystem. Understanding the need and use of these tokens is vital to debug and troubleshoot any configuration issues in a secured Hadoop cluster. In the next chapter we will detail the procedure for securing a Hadoop cluster.

3
Setting Up a Secured Hadoop Cluster

In *Chapter 2*, *Hadoop Security Design*, we looked at the internals of Hadoop security design and enabled ourselves to set up a secured Hadoop cluster. In this chapter, we will look at how to set up a Kerberos authentication and then get into the details of how to set up and configure a secure Hadoop cluster.

To set up a secured Hadoop cluster, we need to set up Kerberos authentication on the nodes. Kerberos authentication requires reverse DNS lookup to work on all the nodes as it uses the hostname to resolve the principal name. Once Kerberos is installed and configured, we set up the Hadoop service principals and all user principals. After that, we update the Hadoop configurations to enable Kerberos authentication on all nodes and start the Hadoop cluster.

These are the topics we'll be covering in this chapter:

- Prerequisites for setting up a secure Hadoop cluster
- Setting up Kerberos
- Configuring Hadoop with Kerberos authentication
- Configuring Hadoop users in a multirealm setup

Prerequisites

The following are the prerequisites for installing a secure Hadoop cluster:

- Root or sudo access for the user installing the cluster.
- Hadoop cluster is configured and running in a non-secured mode.
- Proper file permissions are assigned to local and Hadoop system directories.

- Incase, we are building Kerberos from the source code, we will need the GCC compiler to compile the Kerberos source code. On RHEL/CentOS, run the `yum groupinstall 'Development Tools'` command to install all the dependencies.

- DNS resolutions and host mappings are working for all machines in the cluster. Kerberos doesn't work with IP. Reverse DNS lookup on all nodes should be working and returning the fully qualified hostname.

- The ports required for Kerberos are port 88 for KDC and port 749 for admin services. Since all nodes will have to connect with KDC for authentication, port 88 should be open for all nodes in the cluster running the Hadoop daemons.

- The name of the Kerberos realm that will be used for authenticating the Hadoop cluster.

Setting up Kerberos

The first step in the process to establish a secure Hadoop cluster is to set up the Kerberos authentication and ensure that the Kerberos authentication for the Hadoop service principals are working for all the nodes on the cluster. To set up Kerberos, we establish a Kerberos Server (KDC) on a separate node and install the Kerberos client on all nodes of the Hadoop cluster as shown in the following figure:

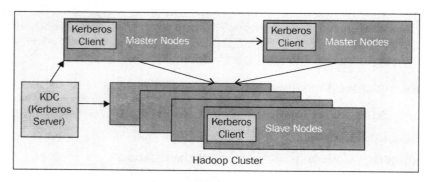

The following figure illustrates the high-level steps involved in installing and configuring Kerberos. It also shows the various Kerberos utilities that are available.

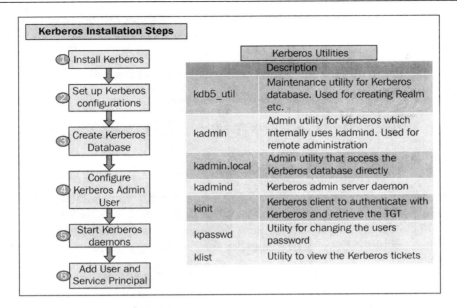

We will use the following realm and domain for the rest of this chapter:

Domain name: `mydomain.com`

Realm name: `MYREALM.COM`

Installing the Key Distribution Center

To set up Kerberos, we need to install the **Key Distribution Center (KDC)** on a secured server.

On RHEL/CentOS/Fedora, to install Kerberos, run the following command with root privileges:

```
yum install krb5-server krb5-libs krb5-workstation
```

Detailed instructions for Kerberos setup is available at the following site:

```
http://www.linuxproblems.org/wiki/Set_up_kerberos_on_Centos_6
```

For Ubuntu distribution, the `apt-get` command to install Kerberos is as follows:

```
sudo apt-get install krb5-kdc krb5-admin-server
```

Detailed instructions to install Kerberos in Ubuntu OS is available at the following site:

```
https://help.ubuntu.com/community/Kerberos
```

There are multiple distributions of the KDC implementations available, and each distribution caters to a specific version and distribution of Linux. If Kerberos needs to be installed from the source, download the latest Kerberos distribution from the MIT website and build the executable using the following procedure:

1. Download Kerberos from `http://web.mit.edu/kerberos/dist/` using the following command:

   ```
   wget http://web.mit.edu/kerberos/dist/krb5/1.10/krb5-1.10.6-
   signed.tar
   ```

2. Unpack the source code and the crypto TAR file to the installation directory using the following command:

   ```
   tar -xvf <downloaded release>
   ```

3. Untar the `krb5-1.11.3.tar.gz` file using the following command:

   ```
   tar -xvf krb5-1.11.3.tar.gz
   ```

4. Go to the `src` directory, configure and compile the source code, and build the executable using the following commands:

   ```
   cd <installation directory>/src
   ```

   ```
   ./configure
   ```

5. After the configuration step, we proceed to make the executable using the following command:

   ```
   make
   ```

 More detailed build configurations and instructions are available at the following URL:

```
http://web.mit.edu/kerberos/krb5-latest/
doc/admin/install_kdc.html#install-and-
configure-the-master-kdc
```

After the KDC installation is completed successfully, the next step is to ensure that the configurations for the KDC are set properly. KDC can be installed as master and slave for fault tolerance. In this setup, we will configure only the master KDC.

Configuring the Key Distribution Center

We will look at Version 5 of MIT Kerberos. This has three configuration files. The krb5.conf file is kept inside /etc/ folder. The kdc.conf and kadm5. acl files are placed inside the /usr/local/var/krb5kdc folder. All of these configuration files follow the Windows INI file format.

krb5.conf is a higher-level configuration and provides the configuration related to the location of KDCs, admin servers, and mappings of hostnames with Kerberos realms. Most of the configurations work with the default values for the current realm and Kerberos application.

The example configuration for the krb5.conf file are provided as follows:

```
[logging]
 default = FILE:/var/log/krb5libs.log
 kdc = FILE:/var/log/krb5kdc.log
 admin_server = FILE:/var/log/kadmind.log


[kdc]
 profile = /usr/local/var/krb5kdc/kdc.conf


[libdefaults]
 default_realm = MYREALM.COM
 dns_lookup_realm = false
 dns_lookup_kdc = false
 ticket_lifetime = 24h
 renew_lifetime = 7d
 forwardable = true
[realms]
 MYREALM.COM = {
  kdc = KerberosServerHostname
  admin_server = KerberosServerHostname
 }
[domain_realm]
 .mydomain.com = MYREALM.COM
 mydomain.com = MYREALM.COM
```

The following table provides the various sections inside the `kdc5.conf` file:

Sr no	Property	Description
1	`libdefaults`	This section contains the default values used by the Kerberos v5 library.
2	`loginproperty"`	This section contains the default values used by the Kerberos v5 login program.
3	`appdefaults`	This section contains the default values that can be used by Kerberos v5 applications.
4	`realms`	This section contains subsections for each of the Kerberos realm. Each subsection describes realm-specific information, including where to find the Kerberos servers for that realm.
5	`domain_realm`	This section contains the relations that map domain names and subdomains with Kerberos realm names. This is used by programs to determine which realm a host should be in, given its fully qualified domain name.
6	`logging`	This section describes the `logging` method used by the various Kerberos programs.
7	`capaths`	This section defines the authentication paths used for cross-realm authentication. This also contains the intermediate realms that are used in a cross-realm authentication.

Some of the Hadoop ecosystem components (Oozie, HUE, and so on) need to renew the Kerberos ticket. So we need to configure KDC to allow renewable tickets. To do this, we add the `renew_lifetime` parameter to the `libdefaults` section of `krb5.conf`.

The `kdc.conf` file contains KDC configuration information related to Kerberos tickets, realm-specific configurations, KDC database, and logging details.

To support renewable tickets, we add the `max_renewable_life` setting to your realm in `kdc.conf`. The key configuration that needs to be set in the `kdc.conf` file is as follows:

```
kdcdefaults]
 kdc_ports = 88

[realms]
MYDOMAIN.COM = {
profile = /etc/krb5.conf
```

```
supported_enctypes = aes128-cts:normal des3-hmac-sha1:normal arcfour-
hmac:normal des-hmac-sha1:normal des-cbc-md5:normal des-cbc-crc:normal
des-cbc-crc:v4 des-cbc-crc:afs3

allow-null-ticket-addresses = true

database_name = /usr/local/var/krb5kdc/principal

acl_file = /usr/local/var/krb5kdc/kadm5.acl

admin_database_lockfile = /usr/local/var/krb5kd/kadm5_adb.lock

admin_keytab = FILE:/usr/local/var/krb5kdc/kadm5.keytab

key_stash_file = /usr/local/var/krb5kdc/.k5stash

kdc_ports = 88

kadmind_port = 749

max_life = 2d 0h 0m 0s

max_renewable_life = 7d 0h 0m 0s
}
```

The following table shows details of the sections that are found in the `kdc.conf` file:

Sr no	Property	Description
1	kdcdefaults	This section contains the default values used for authentication
2	realms	This section contains a separate subsections for every Kerberos realm
3	dbdefaults	This section contains the default database configurations used by KDC for storing the principals
4	dbmodules	This section contains the details for each of the database modules based on the type of database supported
5	logging	This section provides the logging configurations for every Kerberos daemon

Establishing the KDC database

KDC stores the credentials for each of the users in the KDC database. The database can be a file or an LDAP store. To configure a file-based KDC database, we run the following commands using the realm name:

```
kdb5_util create -r MYREALM.COM -s
```

This command will create five files in the `/usr/local/var/krb5kdc` folder:

- The Kerberos database files: `principal` and `principal.ok`
- The Kerberos administrative database file: `principal.kadm5`
- The administrative database lock file: `principal.kadm5.lock`
- The stash file: `.k5.MYREALM.COM.COM`

The stash file is a local copy of the encrypted master key that resides on the KDC's local disk. The stash file is used to automatically authenticate the KDC itself before starting the Kerberos daemons.

Setting up the administrator principal for KDC

Once the KDC database is created, the administrator principal should be configured in the database. To do this, first add the administrator principal in the `/var/Kerberos/krb5kdc/kadm.acl` file that contains the **access control list (ACL)** that is used by the `kadmind` daemon to manage the Kerberos database access.

A typical `kadm.acl` file that provides all administrators with full privilege will have the following entry:

```
*/admin@MYREALM.COM
```

The ACL file follows the following format:

```
principal   permissions   [target_principal   [restrictions] ]
```

The first field in this file is the principal whose permission is set. The permissions specifies what access is granted to the principal. The permissions follow a convention where the uppercase letters deny permission, while the lowercase letters grant the user the requested permissions. Target principal and restrictions are optional fields.

 More details on the various permissions that can be configured can be found at:

```
http://web.mit.edu/kerberos/krb5-latest/
doc/admin/conf_files/kadm5_acl.html
```

Starting the Kerberos daemons

Once the configurations are set properly, we are ready to start the Kerberos daemons.

If Kerberos is installed through `yum` or `apt-get`, the kadmin and KDC server daemon can be started using the following command:

```
service kadmin start
/sbin/service krb5kdc start
```

Krb5kdc is the KDC server, while the kadmin daemon enables administrators to connect from remote machines and perform Kerberos (KDC) administration using the kadmin client.

If Kerberos is installed from the source code, then we use the krb5kdc and kadmind commands to start these daemons in the background, and use logfiles to verify that these daemons have started properly.

Setting up the first Kerberos administrator

Next, we configure the principal password in the KDC database using the kadmin. local command on the master KDC server. Run the following command to set up the administrator principal and provide the password for the administrator principal.

```
kadmin.local -p admin/admin
```

The kinit command is used to authenticate the user with KDC. We can verify the administrator authentication using kinit to ensure that KDC is able to authenticate the users.

```
kinit admin@MYREALM.COM
```

Adding the user or service principals

After the admin user setup is completed and the Kerberos daemons have started, then we can add the principals to the Kerberos database using the kadmin utility.

```
add_principal -randkey user/mydomain.com@MYREALM.COM
```

Configuring LDAP as the Kerberos database

Next we can add the principals to the Kerberos database using the kadmin utility.

```
add_principal -randkey user/mydomain.com@MYREALM.COM
```

Supporting AES-256 encryption for a Kerberos ticket

For some of the operating systems such as CentOS/Red Hat Enterprise Linux 5.6 or later, or Ubuntu with AES-256 encryption, we need to install **Java Cryptography Extension (JCE) Unlimited Strength Jurisdiction Policy File** on all clusters and Hadoop user machines.

More details on JCE can be found at the following link:

```
https://www.owasp.org/index.php/Using_
the_Java_Cryptographic_Extensions
```

Configuring Hadoop with Kerberos authentication

Once the Kerberos setup is completed and the user principals are added to KDC, we can configure Hadoop to use Kerberos authentication. It is assumed that a Hadoop cluster in a non-secured mode is configured and available. We will begin the configuration using Cloudera Distribution of Hadoop (**CDH4**).

The steps involved in configuring Kerberos authentication for Hadoop are shown in the following figure:

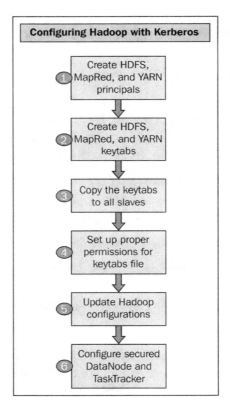

Setting up the Kerberos client on all the Hadoop nodes

In each of the Hadoop node (master node and slave node), we need to install the Kerberos client. This is done by installing the client packages and libraries on the Hadoop nodes.

For RHEL/CentOS/Fedora, we will use the following command:

```
yum install krb5-libs krb5-workstation
```

For Ubuntu, we will use the following command:

```
apt-get install krb5-user
```

Setting up Hadoop service principals

In CDH4, there are three users (`hdfs`, `mapred`, and `yarn`) that are used to run the various Hadoop daemons. All the **Hadoop Distributed File System (HDFS)**-related daemons such as NameNode, DataNode, and Secondary NameNode are run under the `hdfs` user, while for MRV1, the MapReduce-related daemons such as JobTracker and TaskTracker run using the `mapred` user. For MRV2, the `yarn` user runs ResourceManager and NodeManager, while the `mapred` user runs the JobHistory server and the MapReduce application.

We need to create the `hdfs`, `mapred`, and `yarn` principals in KDC to ensure Kerberos authentication for the Hadoop daemons. We have `http` services exposed by all these services, so we need to create a `http` service principal as well. We use the following `kadmin` commands to create these principals:

```
kadmin
kadmin: addprinc -randkey hdfs/mydomain.com@MYREALM.COM
kadmin: addprinc -randkey mapred/mydomain.com@MYREALM.COM
kadmin: addprinc -randkey http/mydomain.com@MYREALM.COM
kadmin: addprinc -randkey yarn/mydomain.com@MYREALM.COM
```

As a part of the Hadoop cluster setup, all the HDFS-related directories that are exclusively used by the `hdfs` daemons such as the NameNode directory, the DataNode directory, and log directories, should have the permissions with `hdfs` as user and group. Also, all folders inside Hadoop and in the local filesystem used by the MapReduce daemons exclusively such as the MapReduce local directory; log directories should have `mapred` as user and group. All directories that are used between `hdfs` and `mapred` daemons should have Hadoop as the user group.

Creating a keytab file for the Hadoop services

A `keytab` is a file containing pairs of Kerberos principals and encrypted keys derived from the Kerberos password. This file is used for headless authentication with KDC when the services run in the background without human intervention. The `keytab` file is created using the `kadmin` commands.

The hdfs and mapred users run multiple Hadoop daemons in background, so we need to create the keytab file for the hdfs and mapred users. We also need to add the http principal to these keytabs, so that the Web UI associated with Hadoop are authenticated using Kerberos.

```
kadmin: xst -norandkey -k hdfs.keytab hdfs/mydomain.com@MYREALM.COM http/
mydomain.com@MYREALM.COM
```

```
kadmin: xst -norandkey -k mapred.keytab hdfs/mydomain.com@MYREALM.COM
http/mydomain.com@MYREALM.COM
```

```
kadmin: xst -norandkey -k yarn.keytab hdfs/mydomain.com@MYREALM.COM http/
mydomain.com@MYREALM.COM
```

Distributing the keytab file for all the slaves

Once the keytab file is created, it has to move to the /etc/hadoop/conf folder. The keytab file has to be secured so that only the owner of keytab can see this file. For this, the hdfs and mapred owner of the keytab file is changed, and the file permission is changed to 400. The service principals for hdfs, mapred, and http has a fully qualified domain name associated with the username. The service principal is host-specific and is unique for each of the nodes in the cluster.

Move the keytab file to the conf folder and secure it

```
$sudo mv hdfs.keytab mapred.keytab /etc/hadoop/conf/
$sudo chown hdfs:hadoop /etc/hadoop/conf/hdfs.keytab
$sudo chown mapred:hadoop /etc/hadoop/conf/mapred.keytab
$sudo chmod 400 /etc/hadoop/conf/hdfs.keytab
$sudo chmod 400 /etc/hadoop/conf/mapred.keytab
```

The keytab file should be created specific to each node in the cluster. Distributing and managing the keytab file in a large cluster is time consuming and error prone. So it is better to use deployment tools and automate this deployment.

Setting up Hadoop configuration files

Next, we update the Hadoop configuration files to enable Kerberos authentication. Before updating the Hadoop configuration file, we should shutdown the cluster.

HDFS-related configurations

The following properties should be updated in the `core-site.xml` file in the `/etc/hadoop/conf` folder. These properties enable Kerberos authentication and user authorization within the Hadoop cluster.

Property name	Value	Description
`hadoop.security.authentication`	`kerberos`	This enables Kerberos authentication for Hadoop
`hadoop.security.authorization`	`true`	This enables authorization in Hadoop to check for file permissions

The `hdfs-site.xml` file should specify the `keytab` file's location, which will be used by the various Hadoop daemons accessing HDFS. The Block Access Token (described in *Chapter 2, Hadoop Security Design*) has to be enabled for HDFS. The configuration should also specify the principal names to be used by the various daemons. Both `http` and `hdfs` principals should be mentioned for each of the daemons (NameNode, DataNode, and Secondary NameNode). Each `hdfs` and `http` principal will be specific to a particular node, and the principal name follows the ensuing convention:

`Name/fullyqualified.domain.name@REALM.COM`

In a Hadoop cluster, there will be thousands of DataNode and it will be impossible to configure the principal manually for each DataNode. So Hadoop provides a `_HOST` variable which gets resolved to the fully-qualified domain name at runtime. This also mandates that the reverse DNS is working properly on all the hosts that are configured this way.

The following properties should be updated in the `hdfs-site.xml` file:

Property name	Value	Description
`dfs.block.access.token.enable`	`true`	This enable security for block access from DataNode
`dfs.namenode.keytab.file`	`/etc/hadoop/conf/hdfs.keytab`	This is the location of the `keytab` file for the `hdfs` user
`dfs.namenode.kerberos.principal`	`hdfs/_HOST@MYREALM.COM`	This is the `hdfs` principal which will be used to start NameNode
`dfs.namenode.kerberos.internal.spnego.principal`	`HTTP/_HOST@MYREALM.COM`	This is the `http` principal for the `http` service

Property name	Value	Description
dfs.secondary.namenode. keytab.file	/etc/hadoop/conf/ hdfs.keytab	This is the location of the keytab file for the hdfs user
dfs.secondary.namenode. kerberos.principal	hdfs/_HOST@ MYREALM.COM	This is the hdfs principal which will be used to start Secondary NameNode
dfs.secondary.namenode. kerberos.internal. spnego.principal	HTTP/_HOST@ MYREALM.COM	This is the http principal for the http service
dfs.datanode.data.dir. perm	700	This is the DataNode directory which should be protected
dfs.datanode.address	0.0.0.0:1004	This DataNode RPC port should be less than 1024
dfs.datanode.http. address	0.0.0.0:1006	This is the DataNode HTTP port which should be less than 1024
dfs.datanode.keytab.file	/etc/hadoop/conf/ hdfs.keytab	This is the location of the keytab file for the hdfs user
dfs.datanode.kerberos. principal	hdfs/_HOST@ MYREALM.COM	This is the http principal for the http service

MRV1-related configurations

For MRV1, the mapred-site.xml file should be configured for securing Hadoop.

The mapred-site.xml file should specify the keytab file's location, which will be used by the JobTracker and TaskTracker daemons. The configurations should also specify the principal names to be used by the various daemons. Each mapred principal will be specific to a particular node. Any user running the MapReduce task also should be configured in each of the nodes on the cluster.

Property name	Value	Description
mapreduce.jobtracker. kerberos.principal	mapred/_HOST@ MYREALM. COM	This is the mapred principal which will be used to start JobTracker
mapreduce.jobtracker. keytab.file	/etc/hadoop/conf/ mapred.keytab	This is the location of the keytab file for the mapred user

Property name	Value	Description
mapreduce. tasktracker.kerberos. principal	mapred/_HOST@ MYREALM. COM	This is the mapred principal which will be used to start TaskTracker
mapreduce. tasktracker.keytab. file	/etc/hadoop/conf/ mapred.keytab	This is the location of the keytab file for the mapred user
mapred.task.tracker. task-controller	org.apache. hadoop.mapred. LinuxTaskController	This is the TaskController class to be used for launching the child JVM
mapreduce. tasktracker.group	mapred	This is the group that runs TaskTracker

MRV2-related configurations

For MRV2, the yarn-site.xml file should be configured for specifying the location of the keytab file of the yarn user for ResourceManager and NodeManager.

Property name	Value	Description
yarn.resourcemanager. keytab	/etc/hadoop/conf/yarn. keytab	This is the location of the keytab file for the yarn user
yarn.resourcemanager. principal	yarn/_HOST@MYREALM.COM	This is the yarn principal name
yarn.nodemanager. keytab	/etc/hadoop/conf/yarn. keytab	This is the location of the keytab file for the yarn user
yarn.nodemanager. principal	yarn/_HOST@MYREALM.COM	This is the yarn principal name
yarn.nodemanager. container-executor. class	org.apache.hadoop. yarn.server. nodemanager. LinuxContainerExecutor	This is the executor class that is launching the applications in yarn
yarn.nodemanager. linux-container- executor.group	yarn	This is the group that is executing Linux containers

The `mapred-site.xml` file should be configured with the `keytab` file location of the job history server. This configuration file should be present in all nodes of the cluster. Each user running the `yarn` jobs should be configured in each of the nodes on the cluster.

Property name	Value	Description
mapreduce. jobhistory.keytab	/etc/hadoop/conf/ mapred.keytab	This is the location of the keytab file for the mapred user
mapreduce. jobhistory.principal	mapred/_HOST@MYREALM. COM	This is the mapred user principal that is used for the JobHistory server

Setting up secured DataNode

Once the Hadoop configuration files are updated, we move to DataNode and ensure it is secured. To do this, we need to start DataNode in a secure mode. **Jsvc** is a set of libraries and applications for making Java applications run on Unix more easily. Jsvc allows the application (for example, Tomcat) to perform some privileged operations as root and then switch to a non-privileged user. This program helps DataNode to bind on ports less than 1024 and then run with the `hdfs` user. The following configurations should be set in each of DataNodes in the `/etc/default/hadoop-hdfs-datanode` folder so that DataNode can run in a secure mode:

```
export HADOOP_SECURE_DN_USER=hdfs

export HADOOP_SECURE_DN_PID_DIR=/var/lib/hadoop-hdfs

export HADOOP_SECURE_DN_LOG_DIR=/var/log/hadoop-hdfs

export JSVC_HOME=/usr/lib/bigtop-utils/ or /usr/libexec/bigtop-utils

(based on the OS the corresponding variable has to be set)
```

Setting up the TaskController class

For MRV1, the `TaskController` class in the Hadoop framework defines how users map and reduce tasks are launched and controlled. For a secured Hadoop cluster, we need to ensure that the user who launched the MapReduce program is running TaskNode. So we need all the users who run the MapReduce program to be defined on all the task nodes. The `TaskController` class uses a setuid executable that is included in the Hadoop distribution to launch and kill tasks on the user's behalf. The `TaskController` class has a configuration file called `task-controller.cfg`. This configuration file is present in the Hadoop configuration folder and uses the key-value pair format. This configuration file should have the following configurations:

Property name	Value	Description
hadoop.log.dir	/var/log/ hadoop- 0.20- mapreduce	Log directory should match the Hadoop log directory. This location is used to give the proper permissions to the user task for writing to this logfile.
mapreduce. tasktracker.group	mapred	Group that the task tracker belongs to.
banned.users	mapred, hdfs, and bin	Users who should be prevented from running MapReduce.
min.user.id	1000	User ID above which will be allowed to run MapReduce.

Once all the configurations are completed, we need to propagate the configuration files to all the slave nodes in the Hadoop cluster.

For MRV2, similar to task-controller.cfg, we need to define container-executor.cfg with the following configurations:

Property name	Value	Description
yarn.nodemanager. linux-container- executor.group	yarn	This is the group that the container belongs to.
yarn.nodemanager.log- dirs	/var/log/ yarn	This log directory should match to the Hadoop log directory. This location is used to give the proper permissions to the user task for writing in this logfile.
banned.users	hdfs, yarn, mapred, and bin	These are the users who should be prevented from running MapReduce.
min.user.id	1000	This is the user ID value above which will be allowed to run MapReduce.

We can then start all the Hadoop daemons using the following commands:

```
sudo service hadoop-hdfs-namenode start
sudo service hadoop-hdfs-datanode start
sudo service hadoop-hdfs-secondarynamenode start
```

For MRV1:

```
sudo service hadoop-0.20-mapreduce-jobtracker start
```

For MRV2:

```
sudo service hadoop-yarn-resourcemanager start
sudo service hadoop-yarn-nodemanager start
sudo service hadoop-mapreduce-historyserver start
```

After the startup, verify the output looking at the logfile of the various daemons to ensure that the `security.UserGroupInformation` entry within the logfile shows the authentication performed for the Kerberos principal, for example:

```
INFO security.UserGroupInformation:
Login successful for user hdfs/mydomain.com@MYREALM.COM using keytab file
/etc/hadoop/conf/hdfs.keytab
```

Configuring users for Hadoop

All users required to run MapReduce jobs on the cluster need to be set up all the nodes in the cluster. In a large cluster, setting up these users will be very time consuming. So the best practice is to integrate the existing enterprise users in Active Directory or LDAP using cross-realm authentication in Kerberos.

Users are centrally managed in Active Directory or LDAP, and we set up a one-way cross-realm trust between Active Directory/LDAP and KDC on the cluster. Thus, the Hadoop service principal doesn't have to be set up in Active Directory/LDAP, and they authenticate locally on the cluster with KDC. This also ensures that the cluster load is isolated from the rest of the enterprise. We look at how to integrate Hadoop security with **Enterprise Security Systems** in subsequent chapters.

Automation of a secured Hadoop deployment

In a production environment, there are hundreds (sometimes even thousands) of nodes in a Hadoop cluster. Managing and configuring such a large cluster is not done manually as it is laborious and error prone. Traditionally, enterprises used Chef/Puppet or a similar solution for cluster configuration management and deployment, In this approach, organizations had to continuously update their chef recipes based on the changes in Apache Hadoop releases. Instead, organizations typically deploy Hadoop cluster deployment automation based on the Hadoop distribution they work with. For example, in a Cloudera-based Hadoop distribution, organizations leverages **Cloudera Manager** to provide cluster deployment. automation, and management capability. For Hortonworks-based distributions, organizations prefer Ambari. Similarly, Intel distribution has **Intel Manager** for Apache Hadoop. Each of these deployment managers support secured Hadoop deployment. The approach and details to configure the security remains the same; however, these tools provide the automation required for seamless deployment of the secured Hadoop cluster.

Summary

In this chapter, we looked at the steps to set up the Kerberos authentication protocol and how to add the required principals to the KDC. We then looked at the overall process of configuring the Hadoop security with Kerberos. The Hadoop configurations have to be replicated in all the nodes of the cluster. All users running MapReduce need to set up on all nodes of the cluster. Setting up users across the entire cluster nodes can be challenging and setting up an Active Directory- or LDAP-based authentication mechanism avoids the problem of manually creating the users in each of the cluster nodes.

In the next chapter, we will look at how we can configure Kerberos security for the rest of the Hadoop ecosystem such as Hive, WebHDFS, Oozie, and Flume.

4
Securing the Hadoop Ecosystem

In *Chapter 3, Setting Up a Secured Hadoop Cluster*, we looked at how to set up Kerberos authentication for HDFS and MapReduce components within a secured Hadoop cluster. But in our secured Big Data journey, this is only half done. The Hadoop ecosystem consists of various components such as Hive, Oozie, and HBase. We need to secure all the other Hadoop ecosystem components. In this chapter, we will look at the each of the ecosystem components and the various security challenges for each of these components, and how to set up secured authentication and user authorization for each of them.

Each ecosystem component has its own security challenges and needs to be configured uniquely based on its architecture to secure them. Each of these ecosystem components has end users directly accessing the component or a backend service accessing the Hadoop core components (HDFS and MapReduce).

The following are the topics that we'll be covering in this chapter:

- Configuring authentication and authorization for the following Hadoop ecosystem components:
  - Hive
  - Oozie
  - Flume
  - HBase
  - Sqoop
  - Pig

- Best practices in configuring secured Hadoop components

Configuring Kerberos for Hadoop ecosystem components

The Hadoop ecosystem is growing continuously and maturing with increasing enterprise adoption. In this section, we look at some of the most important Hadoop ecosystem components, their architecture, and how they can be secured.

Securing Hive

Hive provides the ability to run SQL queries over the data stored in the HDFS. Hive provides the Hive query engine that converts Hive queries provided by the user to a pipeline of MapReduce jobs that are submitted to Hadoop (JobTracker or ResourceManager) for execution. The results of the MapReduce executions are then presented back to the user or stored in HDFS. The following figure shows a high-level interaction of a business user working with Hive to run Hive queries on Hadoop:

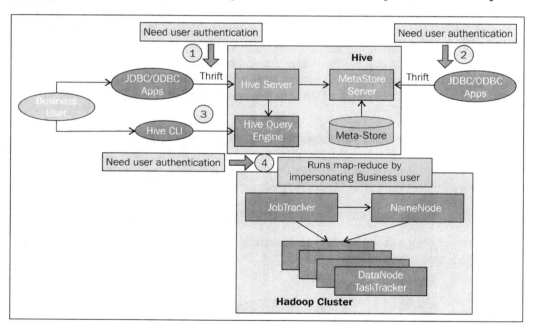

There are multiple ways a Hadoop user can interact with Hive and run Hive queries; these are as follows:

- The user can directly run the Hive queries using **Command Line Interface (CLI)**. The CLI connects to the Hive metastore using the metastore server and invokes Hive query engine directly to execute Hive query on the cluster.

- Custom applications written in Java and other languages interacts with Hive using the **HiveServer**. HiveServer, internally, uses the metastore server and the Hive Query Engine to execute the Hive query on the cluster.

To secure Hive in the Hadoop ecosystem, the following interactions should be secured:

- User interaction with Hive CLI or HiveServer
- User roles and privileges needs to be enforced to ensure users have access to only authorized data
- The interaction between Hive and Hadoop (JobTracker or ResourceManager) has to be secured and the user roles and privileges should be propagated to Hadoop jobs

To ensure secure Hive user interaction, there is a need to ensure that the user is authenticated by HiveServer or CLI before running any jobs on the cluster. The user has to first use the `kinit` command to fetch the Kerberos ticket. This ticket is stored in the credential cache and used to authenticate with Kerberos-enabled systems.

Once the user is authenticated, Hive submits the job to Hadoop (JobTracker or ResourceManager). Hive needs to impersonate the user to execute MapReduce on the cluster. From Hive Version 0.11 onwards, HiveServer2 was introduced. The earlier HiveServer had serious security limitations related to user authentication.

HiveServer2 supports Kerberos and LDAP authentication for the user authentication.

When HiveServer2 is configured to have LDAP authentication, Hive users are managed using the LDAP store. Hive asks the users to submit the MapReduce jobs to Hadoop. Thus, if we configure HiveServer2 to use LDAP, only the user authentication between the client and HiveServer2 is addressed. The interaction of Hive with Hadoop is insecure, and Hive MapReduce will be able to access other users' data in the Hadoop cluster.

On the other hand, when we use Kerberos authentication for Hive users with HiveServer2, the same user is impersonated to execute MapReduce on the Hadoop cluster. So it is recommended that in a production environment, we configure HiveServer2 with Kerberos to have a seamless authentication and access control for the users submitting Hive queries. The credential store for Kerberos KDC can be configured to be LDAP so that we can centrally manage the user credentials of the end users.

To set up a secured Hive interactions, we need to do the following steps:

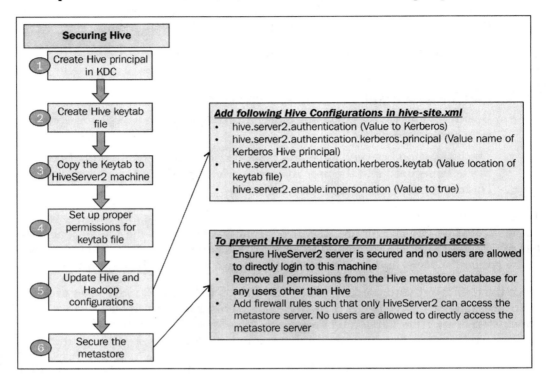

One of the key steps in securing Hive interaction is to ensure that the Hive user is impersonated in Hadoop, as Hive executes a MapReduce job on the Hadoop cluster. To achieve this goal, we need to add the `hive.server2.enable.impersonation` configuration in `hive-site.xml`, and `hadoop.proxyuser.hive.hosts` and `hadoop.proxyuser.hive.groups` in `core-site.xml`.

```
<property>
<name>hive.server2.authentication</name>
<value>KERBEROS</value>
</property>
<property>
<name>hive.server2.authentication.kerberos.principal</name>
<value>hive/_HOST@YOUR-REALM.COM</value>
</property>
<property>
```

```
<name>hive.server2.authentication.kerberos.keytab</name>
<value>/etc/hive/conf/hive.keytab</value>
</property>
<property>
<name>hive.server2.enable.impersonation</name>
<description>Enable user impersonation for
HiveServer2</description>
<value>true</value>
</property>
```

Securing Hive using Sentry

In the previous section, we saw how Hive authentication can be enforced using Kerberos and the user privileges that are enforced by using user impersonation in Hadoop by the superuser.

Sentry is the one of the latest entrant in the Hadoop ecosystem that provides fine-grained user authorization for the data that is stored in Hive. Sentry provides fine-grained, role-based authorization to Hive and **Impala**. Sentry uses HiveServer2 and metastore server to execute the queries on the Hadoop platform. However, the user impersonation is turned off in HiveServer2 when Sentry is used. Sentry enforces user privileges on the Hadoop data using the Hive metastore. Sentry supports authorization policies per database/schema. This could be leveraged to enforce user management policies.

> More details on Sentry are available at the following URL:
>
> http://www.cloudera.com/content/cloudera/
> en/products/cdh/sentry.html

Securing Oozie

Usually in a production system, there is a need to run a series of heterogeneous tasks consisting of Pig, Hive, MapReduce, and so on in some predefined sequence. To achieve this we use Oozie. Oozie is a workflow orchestrator and scheduler for the Hadoop ecosystem. Oozie takes an input XML configuration file that contains information about the sequence and dependency from the user, and executes a workflow of jobs that may contain Hive, Pig, MapReduce, Java, or shell scripts.

The following figure shows the interaction of a user executing tasks on Oozie:

End users access Oozie through **Web Browser** (Oozie web client) or **Java Client** (custom Java code written to connect and submit jobs to Oozie) or **Oozie CLI**. Each of these entry points needs to enforce user authentication and authorization. Refer to **1, 2, 3** in the preceding figure.

Oozie executes the jobs on the Hadoop cluster on behalf of the end user. This needs the Oozie user to impersonate the end user on the Hadoop cluster. This ensures that the end user's access privileges are used by the jobs during the execution, and only the folders authorized for the end user are allowed to be accessed. These jobs are scheduled and they will execute the job task long after the user has submitted the job to Oozie. This means Oozie should be able to renew any authentication ticket it has got from the user when it submits the job to Hadoop. Refer to **4** in the preceding figure.

Oozie stores all the job information and status information in the **Metastore**. So it needs to authenticate the Oozie user to the **Metastore**.

To secure Oozie, we need to secure two different interactions. First we look at the approach to authenticate end users while accessing Oozie securely. Next we look at how the Oozie server is going to run jobs on a secured Hadoop cluster.

To ensure secure end users are accessing Oozie web applications, Oozie provides user authentication to the Oozie web services. Oozie supports HTTPS (SSL)-base encryption between Oozie server and browser.

Oozie also provides Kerberos HTTP **Simple and Protected GSSAPI Negotiation Mechanism (SPNEGO)** authentication for web clients. SPNEGO protocol is used when a client application wants to authenticate to a remote server, but is not sure of the authentication protocols to use. For Oozie web clients, we need to set up SPNEGO authentication on the user browser. In each browser, there is a unique way to configure SPNEGO:

- For the IE browser, to turn on SPNEGO, we turn on **Windows Integrated Authentication** and add the URL to the local intranet sites

- For Firefox, in the **about:config** page, configure `network.negotiate-auth.trusted-uris` to the Oozie server hostname

- For Chrome browser, run the following command:

```
C:\Users\username\AppData\Local\Google\Chrome\Application\chrome.
exe --args --auth-server whitelist="*mydomain.com" --auto-ssl-
client-auth
```

Compared to SPNEGO, HTTPS (SSL)-based encryption can also be used to securely communicate with browser client and server.

To set up Oozie on a secured Hadoop cluster, we add the Oozie principal in KDC and use this Oozie user to start the Oozie application. Oozie user is configured as a superuser in Hadoop. This allows an Oozie user to impersonate end users. Hadoop limits the list of groups that will be allowed to be impersonated by the Oozie superuser in `core-site.xml`. Also, we set the list of host machines through which the Oozie superuser is going to connect to Hadoop and impersonate the end user. Hadoop only authenticates the Oozie user, and it is the responsibility of Oozie application to authenticate the end user and ensure that only authenticated users are given access to submit the job to Hadoop.

We adopt the steps mentioned in the following figure to set up a secured Oozie in the Hadoop cluster:

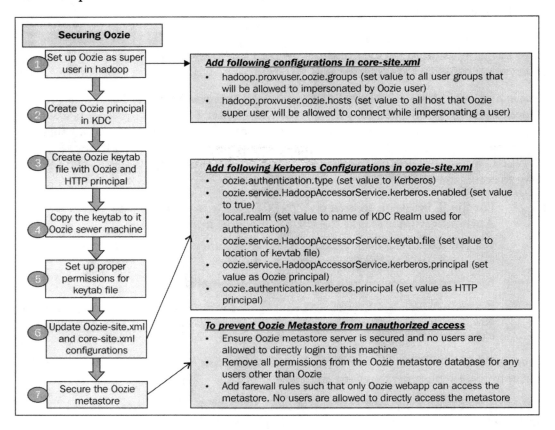

Securing Flume

Flume is a distributed, reliable, near real-time ingestion component in the Hadoop ecosystem. We will narrow our focus to the latest version of Flume known as Flume-ng. Flume has the concepts of **Source**, **Channel**, and **Sink** to ensure reliable communication. All these are embedded in a single **Flume Agent**. Source collects the events from the various source systems and pushes it to the channel. The channel is usually implemented using file, RDBMS, or memory. **Sink** pushes data to the target system. **Channel** removes the data once the sink is able to successfully deliver the event to the target system. Thus, there are multiple handshakes as data is ingested from multiple **Source System** through Flume.

In Hadoop, `core-site.xml` specifies Flume as a superuser and establishes the group of users that will be impersonated by Flume, with the help of the following configuration:

```
<property>
<name>hadoop.proxyuser.flume.groups</name>
<value>*</value>
</property>
<property>
<name>hadoop.proxyuser.flume.hosts</name>
<value>*</value>
</property>
```

We can restrict the groups that are impersonated and the hosts that can establish a connection with Hadoop by providing the values for groups and hosts instead of using *.

Securing a Flume channel

Flume supports memory, database, and file channels. Data security is a concern only for database and file channels as the data is persisted external to the process running the Flume agent. Database channel provides user authentication and authorization controls using the standard database security mechanism and the username and password can be provided in `connection.properties.file`. File channels provides security using encryption of the data stored in the file. File channels support data encryption using the Java keystores.

For details on the properties for configuring Flume file channels with encryption, refer to `http://flume.apache.org/FlumeUserGuide.html` and navigate to the File Channel configurations.

Securing HBase

HBase is a column-oriented, distributed NoSQL database that uses HDFS as the distributed filesystem for storing the data. HBase leverage **ZooKeeper** as the coordination services and stores the information about the HBase cluster. There are two types of cluster nodes in a HBase cluster (**Master** and **RegionServer**). The Master manages the organization of the data stored in HBase, while each RegionServer in HBase hosts multiple Regions. **Region** is responsible for managing the data and it resides within RegionServer.

For any client to write or read data from HBase, it needs to have connectivity with ZooKeeper and RegionServers. Client first contacts the ZooKeeper to fetch the information on where the keys are located and then it contacts the corresponding RegionServer to fetch the data. The RegionServer delegates the request to the correct Region, which finally returns the data to the client.

The data residing in a particular Region is persisted in HDFS. Thus, HBase daemons in the RegionServer communicate with HDFS (NameNode) to store the data. The HBase Master communicates with ZooKeeper to store the cluster details and Region metadata. As shown in the following figure, there are two interactions that needs to be secured to establish a secured HBase cluster. First, the HBase end users should be authenticated with HBase. Second, the HBase daemons need to securely authenticate itself with ZooKeeper and Hadoop. Apart from this, the data residing in the RegionServer should be secured.

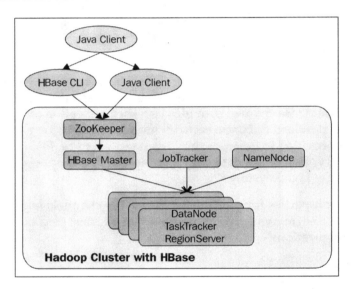

To set up a secured HBase cluster, the procedure mentioned in the following figure needs to be followed:

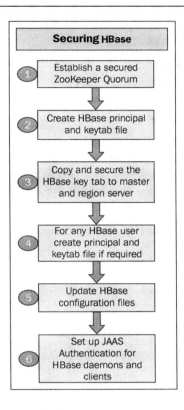

To secure the HBase daemons, the HBase configuration file `/etc/hbase/conf/hbase-site.xml`, needs to be updated with the following properties:

```
<property>
<name>hbase.security.authentication</name>
<value>kerberos</value>
</property>
<property>
<name>hbase.rpc.engine</name>
<value>org.apache.hadoop.hbase.ipc.SecureRpcEngine</value>
</property>
<property>
<name>hbase.regionserver.kerberos.principal</name>
<value>hbase/_HOST@MYREALM.COM</value>
</property>
<property>
<name>hbase.regionserver.keytab.file</name>
<value>/etc/hbase/conf/hbase.keytab</value>
</property>
<property>
```

```
<name>hbase.master.kerberos.principal</name>
<value>hbase/_HOST@MYREALM.COM</value>
</property>
<property>
<name>hbase.master.keytab.file</name>
<value>/etc/hbase/conf/hbase.keytab</value>
</property>
```

For user authentication, one of the preferred way is for the HBase Java client and HBase daemons to use **Java Authentication and Authorization Service (JAAS)**. To establish this secured authentication we need to configure JAAS configuration file /etc/hbase/conf/hbase-jaas.conf with the following details:

```
Client {
  com.sun.security.auth.module.Krb5LoginModule required
  useKeyTab=true
useTicketCache=false
  keyTab="/etc/hbase/conf/hbase.keytab"
  principal="hbase/mydomain.com@MYREALM.COM";
};
```

Then export the following JVM options so that JAAS authentication is enforced:

```
export HBASE_OPTS="$HBASE_OPTS -Djava.security.auth.login.config=/etc/
hbase/conf/hbase-jaas.conf"
```

This will ensure that the HBase daemons and HBase client uses the specified keytab to authenticate itself with KDC and obtain the Kerberos ticket.

Apart from service authentication, HBase also provides user authorization on tables, column families, and column qualifiers. Authorization is not currently supported at row level or cell level. To secure a particular table in HBase, we use the Grant command in HBase shell. Apart from this, there are commands to alter, revoke, and view user permissions. These commands are used to secure the HBase tables, column families, and column qualifiers across users. The following are the permissions supported by HBase:

Permission	Description
R	This allows to perform get, scan, or exists commands
W	This allows to perform put, delete, lockRow, unlockRow,incrementColumnValue, checkAndDelete,checkAndPut, flush, or compact
C	This allows to perform create, alter, or drop commands
A	This is the admin permissions that allows to perform enable, disable, majorCompact, grant, revoke, and shutdown commands

For example, to grant `delete` and `create` table permissions on a particular column qualifier, the following command has to be executed in HBase shell:

```
grant user WC table columnfamily columqualifier
```

The user authorization is implemented using coprocessors. Coprocessors are like database triggers in HBase. They intercept any request to the table before and after. These hookpoints are used to implement table-level security. So we need to add the following settings to enable security-related coprocessors in HBase:

```
<property>
<name>hbase.security.authorization</name>
<value>true</value>
</property>
<property>
<name>hbase.coprocessor.master.classes</name>
<value>org.apache.hadoop.hbase.security.access.AccessController
</value>
</property>
<property>
<name>hbase.coprocessor.region.classes</name>
<value>org.apache.hadoop.hbase.security.token.TokenProvider,
org.apache.hadoop.hbase.security.access.AccessController
</value>
</property>
```

Securing Sqoop

Sqoop is used for bulk transfer of data between structured sources such as RDBMS, NoSQL, and Hadoop. The initial version of Sqoop known as Sqoop1 was built as a command-line client tool that generated the MapReduce code based on the metadata retrieved from a structured store such as RDBMS. The connection parameters are provided as arguments in the command line and the credentials for the user running the Sqoop command was used to submit the job to Hadoop. In this version, there is no secure way to protect the user credentials as Sqoop expects clear text password. So this version when used in a production scenario, creates a big security hole as the passwords used for the Sqoop commands are plain text passwords kept in some properties file.

While using Sqoop1 with secure Hadoop cluster, the user running the Sqoop command needs to have a valid Kerberos ticket so that this ticket can be used to authenticate with JobTracker and NameNode.

The key limitations of Sqoop 1 are as follows:

The credentials used for connecting to the database are plain text and specified in the properties file Sqoop supports code generation, and this generated code can be compromised by any malicious user to run any MapReduce code in the cluster

Sqoop2 was developed to address these limitations of Sqoop. Sqoop2 is a client server-based model, where the database credentials are managed centrally in the server with role-based authentication. The administrator of Sqoop2 manages the various database connection credentials and provides the connection name which is used by the Sqoop2 user. Thus, the user of Sqoop2 doesn't need to know the database credentials for the database. There is a role-based security for the database connections which defines the user-specific access to the Sqoop2 database connection. The users are provided access to various database connections and they reference those connections in the Sqoop commands. Sqoop2 also limited the code-generated capability to the end users. Sqoop2 doesn't support client users to be propagated to Hadoop by impersonation. Sqoop users are independently authenticated by Sqoop2 and they internally access the required databases using the credentials provided in the connection, and uses Sqoop user ID to authenticate with Hadoop and submit the job on the secured cluster. Sqoop2 jobs are submitted under the Sqoop user ID and not using the user account. This is one of the security concern in using Sqoop2, as the user privileges are not enforced in Hadoop when the user is performing Sqoop operations using Sqoop2. This is planned to be addressed in the future releases of Sqoop2.

Thus, there is no support for Sqoop2 with Kerberos security by default. The user starting the Sqoop2 service needs to obtain the Kerberos ticket using kinit from keytab and then set up a process to renew the ticket periodically.

Securing Pig

Similar to Hive, Pig provides user the ability to write the logic in procedural way in language known as Pig Latin, and then Pig converts this logic to a pipeline of MapReduce jobs and executes on the Hadoop cluster.

Pig uses the user credentials to submit the job to Hadoop. So there is no need of any additional Kerberos security authentication. Pig users need to have a valid Kerberos ticket which is obtained by running kinit. So before starting Pig, the user should authenticate with KDC and obtain a valid Kerberos ticket. The following are the steps to access Pig in a secured Hadoop cluster:

1. User logs into the machine where Pig is installed with the user credentials.
2. User performs a kinit operation and gets the Kerberos **ticket-granting ticket (TGT)** for the user.

3. When the user invokes Pig Grunt or runs the Pig script, Hadoop fetches the ticket from the ticket cache and uses it for authentication.

Best practices for securing the Hadoop ecosystem components

We looked at different types of Hadoop ecosystem components and understood how to set up a secured Hadoop ecosystem with all these components. In this section, let us summarize these best practices as follows:

- All services that are running within the Hadoop ecosystem need to be authenticated with KDC. This will ensure that there is no rogue process creating malicious activity.

- It is a best practice to store the KDC credentials in an LDAP store, so that the credentials and authorizations can be centrally managed.

- The keytab file needs to be secured, and only the user for whom the file is created should be provided with read access to the file.

- Whenever a Java client is accessing the service, client authentication should be done by the service using RPC authentication mechanism.

- Whenever user impersonation is used to impersonate an end user by the service user, the service process has to be fully secured by Kerberos and also the host running the service should have limited user access. User authentication is crucial as any security lapse might result in a malicious user impersonating any other valid user.

- Whenever Hadoop services are acting on end user's behalf, it is better to run the operation as the request user by impersonation. This will ensure that only the user-permitted operations are allowed.This ensures that the job has only the user privileges within the cluster.

- To run secured authentication in JVM, we can use the JAAS file to perform the authentication.

- Enforce strict firewall rules on the cluster to ensure that there is no unauthorized access. Organizations usually restrict all traffic by configuring a secured VLAN for the Hadoop cluster. The firewall rules are imposed on the VLAN to ensure that there are no connections initiated from unknown sources to the Hadoop cluster. All connections are limited to be initiated from the gateway servers residing on the edge of the Hadoop cluster. More details on this will be discussed in *Chapter 5, Integrating Hadoop with Enterprise Security Systems*.

Summary

In this chapter, we looked at the steps that need to be adopted to set up various Hadoop ecosystem components. At the high level, the process involves creating the Kerberos principal for each of the components and then securing the keytab file under the user's home directory. If the service has to impersonate the end user, then the service principal is configured as superuser in Hadoop. Each ecosystem component has specific configuration that needs to be updated to support secured authentication with Kerberos. Some of the components such as Sqoop or Sqoop2, leave a certain amount of security hole when used in production. So these components have to be used with caution and deployed with additional security measures.

In the next chapter, we will look at how to integrate the authentication and authorization of these ecosystem components with the Enterprise Identity Management systems.

5
Integrating Hadoop with Enterprise Security Systems

In the previous chapter, we looked at how to establish Kerberos authentication for the Hadoop ecosystem components. Establishing the authentication is only the first step towards providing secured access to the Hadoop ecosystem. In this chapter, we will focus on centrally managing the authentication and authorization of the various Hadoop users, and address the various challenges for integrating the Enterprise Security Systems with a secured Hadoop cluster.

Once Hadoop users are centrally managed, there is a need for these users to directly access and work on the Hadoop cluster. However, Hadoop service daemons use multiple communication protocols to communicate with each other. This requires multiple unsecured ports to be opened between the cluster machines. This brings in a security concern for the organization deploying Hadoop. So, usually, Hadoop clusters are isolated in a separate network and user access is only provided through some servers residing on the edge of the network known as EdgeNodes, or JumpServers, or Gateways. EdgeNodes and Gateways are servers positioned on the edge of the Hadoop cluster that allows connectivity to both the Hadoop cluster and the corporate networks. Hadoop users have to log in to EdgeNodes or Gateways and then access the Hadoop resources and services. This is usually one of the concerns for end users as every user operation usually involves two steps: firstly, copying the required files to the Gateway server, and then executing the Hadoop operations from the Gateway server. We will look at the various solutions available today to directly access the Hadoop cluster from the corporate network without directly logging into the Gateway server.

These are the topics we'll be covering in this chapter:

- Integrating Enterprise Identity Management Systems with the Hadoop ecosystem
- Accessing secured Hadoop cluster resources from corporate networks

Integrating Enterprise Identity Management systems

Typically, organizations have a central user identity management system known as **Enterprise Identity Management (EIM)** system using products such as IBM Tivoli Identity Manager, Oracle Identity Manager, and Windows Active Directory. Enterprise user's access privileges are centrally managed in these systems. These systems manage the user credentials and their roles using groups. User authorization is managed using these security groups. Users are assigned to groups, where each group has a specific authorization and access privilege defined. The user inherits group privileges based on their group membership.

By default, Hadoop uses the logged in **Operating System (OS)** users and the corresponding user groups to provide the authorization within Hadoop. Hadoop daemons (NameNode, DataNode, and so on) and ecosystem components such as Oozie, Hive, HBase uses these group memberships to determine the level of authorization allowed for the user. By default, this is set to the user's OS groups defined in the Linux system. However in a large cluster, this default configuration to fetch the OS users and corresponding groups is not a scalable solution. We need to manage the users and their roles centrally in the EIM systems.

To manage the user's credentials and roles in an EIM system, follow these steps:

- Hadoop end users are defined with in the EIM system. User credentials are centrally managed by the EIM system. As Hadoop uses Kerberos for user authentication in a secured Hadoop cluster, EIM system should support Kerberos authentication and issue a Kerberos ticket for the end users. This user ticket will be used for authentication and access to the Hadoop resources. The user IDs of these Hadoop users should be mapped to the corresponding user principals defined in Kerberos using the mapping rules in Hadoop.
- User groups defined in the EIM systems needs be used by the Hadoop daemons for authorization. In a typical production setup, user and user group information is synchronized between EIM systems and the Hadoop local KDC so that Hadoop daemons don't have to contact the EIM systems for group information and can get this user group information from the LDAP servers defined locally.

- We only defined the Hadoop end users in the EIM system and not the Hadoop service daemon users such as HDFS, MapRed, or YARN. The users running the Hadoop service daemons are defined in the local KDC residing in the Hadoop cluster.

- Here is the high-level interaction of a corporate user with in the Hadoop cluster using EIM system security within a secured Hadoop cluster:

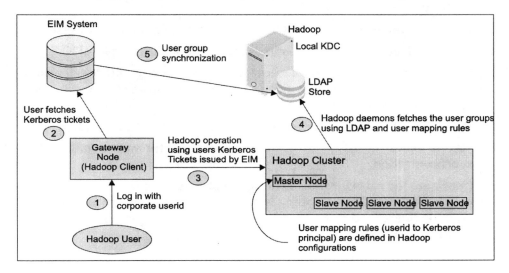

1. First, the user authenticates with the EIM system using the user credentials.

2. The EIM system issues the Kerberos ticket to the user after authentication.

3. Then the user presents this ticket to Hadoop to perform operations on the secured Hadoop cluster. The Hadoop daemons trust the EIM system, issue ticket due to the cross-realm trust established between Hadoop local KDC and the EIM system.

4. The Hadoop daemon fetches the user group information from LDAP to provide the authorized access to the user. If the user IDs and the Kerberos principals are not the same, the mapping of the user ID to Kerberos principal is defined in the `core-site.xml`.

5. To ensure that there is a centralized management of user credentials and roles, there is a need to synchronize the user groups between the EIM system and the local KDC. Only the roles and groups are synchronized and user credentials are stored only in the EIM system.

6. To ensure that the Hadoop daemons authenticate the end user using the Kerberos ticket issued by the EIM system, we need to establish the cross-realm trust between the Hadoop local KDC and the EIM system.

Configuring EIM integration with Hadoop

To implement integration between the EIM system and the Hadoop local KDC, follow these steps:

1. Set up one-way trust between EIM systems and the local KDC.

2. Set up realm details for EIM and local KDC in all the nodes on the cluster to enable cross-realm authentication.

3. Set up all end users, their credentials, and their roles in the EIM system.

4. Set up all Hadoop service principals and credentials in the local KDC.

5. Set up the synchronization of roles/groups between the EIM system and local KDC. This can be done using LDAP synchronization connectors such as **LDAP Synchronization Connector (LSC)**.

6. Refer to the LSC project for more details on LDAP Synchronization.

7. Have a look at `http://lsc-project.org/wiki/` for more details on LDAP synchronization.

8. Configure the rules for transforming the principals to the corresponding user in Kerberos. This mapping is provided by the property `hadoop.security.auth_to_local` in `core-site.xml`. A simple rule will be of the form as follows:

`hadoop.security.auth_to_local`

```
RULE:[1:$1@$0](.*@MYREALM)s/@.*//
RULE:[2:$1@$0](hdfs@.*MYREALM)s/.*/hdfs/
DEFAULT
```

 More details on how to set this rule are available at:

`http://www.cloudera.com/content/cloudera-content/cloudera-docs/CDH4/4.2.1/CDH4-Security-Guide/cdh4sg_topic_19.html`

Integrating Active-Directory-based EIM with the Hadoop ecosystem

Let us look in detail at how we integrate an Active Directory-based EIM system with a Hadoop cluster which has MIT Kerberos as the local KDC in a Windows machine where Active Directory is installed.

1. Add the Hadoop local KDC to the Active Directory hosting the user realm.

   `ksetup /addkdc MYREALM.COM kdc-server MYCORPORATEDOMAIN.COM`

2. Add trust between the two KDC.

```
netdom trust MYREALM.COM /Domain:MYCORPORATEDOMAIN.COM /add /realm
/passwordt:<myPasswordforcrossrealm>
```

3. Set up the encryption protocol for communication between local realm and Active Directory.

```
ktpass /MITRealmName MYREALM.COM /TrustEncryp <enc_type>
```

4. Add user principals in the Active Directory.

```
kadmin:  addprinc -e "rc4-hmac:normal des3-hmac-sha1:normal"
krbtgt/mycorporatedomain.com@MYCORPORATEDOMAIN.COM
```

5. Add Hadoop service principals in the Local KDC.

```
kadmin:  addprinc -e "rc4-hmac:normal des3-hmac-sha1:normal"
krbtgt/mydomain.com@MYREALM.COM
```

6. Establish the synchronization of user groups between the Active Directory and local KDC using the LDAP synchronization connector.

Accessing a secured Hadoop cluster from an enterprise network

Typical deployment architecture of a secured Hadoop cluster in an enterprise context is shown in the following diagram:

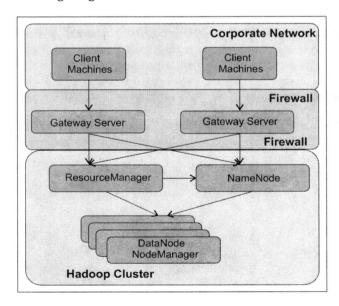

The **Corporate Network** is firewalled with the Hadoop cluster and connectivity is only provided through the EdgeNodes (also also known as Gateway Servers). The **Gateway Server** allows an entry point for external applications, tools, and users to the secured Hadoop cluster. It is deployed between the Hadoop cluster and the corporate network. As all users log in to this machine and the credentials for the user defined in this machine are used while accessing the Hadoop cluster, this node can be used to provide access control, policy enforcement, logging, and gateway services to the Hadoop environment. Depending on the number of users accessing the Hadoop cluster, there could be more than one Gateway Server in a Hadoop cluster.

Clients in the corporate network can't directly access the Hadoop cluster. They log in to the Gateway Servers and perform all the operations on the Hadoop cluster. All client tools such as Hive, Pig, Oozie, and so on, are installed on the Gateway Servers so that users need not be provided login access to every node on the cluster and the cluster nodes are secured from any unauthorized access. Also, these tools have connectivity to every machine on the cluster.

Clients would like to have direct access to submit jobs or browse files on the Hadoop cluster from the corporate network without logging in to the Gateway Server.

There are multiple solutions to address this problem such as HttpFS, HUE, and Knox Gateway. Each one has its own merits and demerits. Let's look at each one of them.

HttpFS

One solution to provide direct access for Hadoop operations from the corporate network is by installing HttpFS on the Gateway Servers of the cluster. HttpFS can be used to access data in HDFS on a cluster behind a firewall. HttpFS is a Java-based web application and it runs using a preconfigured Tomcat bundled with HttpFS binary distribution. It acts as a HTTP proxy that authenticates the clients and then proxies the client to access the files on the cluster. It internally uses WebHDFS to access the cluster resources.

To set up secured access to a Hadoop cluster, HttpFS should be configured to use Kerberos security. The steps shown in the following figure are required to configure HttpFS in secured mode:

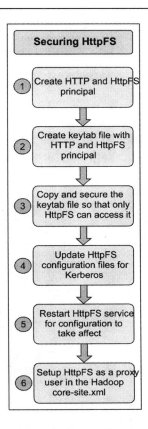

HttpFS acts as a proxy and uses WebHDFS to store data in the cluster. One of the biggest limitations of HttpFS is that we can't transfer large volumes of data through this HTTP interface. HttpFS runs as a Tomcat-based web application and the data has to move through this application when we transfer the data to the cluster. We should use the native RPC to transfer large volume of data.

HttpFS only provides access to work with **Hadoop Distributed File System (HDFS)**. When user needs to run Pig, Hive, MapReduce on the cluster, they still need to log in to the Gateway Server.

HUE

HUE is the open source Apache Hadoop UI. HUE provides the web application to perform the following tasks:

- Browse the HDFS filesystem
- Develop workflows that can be submitted to Oozie

- Pig editor and executor
- Job browser for MapReduce jobs running on the secured Hadoop cluster
- UI to submit query for Hive, Impala
- Scoop command executor

One of the limitations of HUE is for file uploads and downloads from the Hadoop cluster. HUE uses HttpFS internally to proxy the Hadoop cluster when installed on the Gateway Server. The following diagram shows the interaction of the end users using HUE:

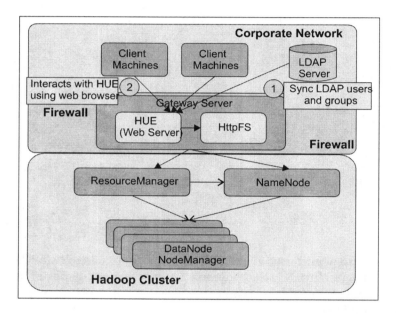

HUE provides the ability to authenticate users using corporate Identity Manager. It provides the ability to synchronize users and groups using LDAP's **Add/synch** feature. Thus, the corporate users can be managed centrally through the Enterprise Identity Manager. HUE provides access through granular control of the group's access privileges. HUE provides secured authentication of the users using SPNEGO-based browser authentication. User access to HUE from the corporate network is secured over a HTTPS connection. For HTTPS access, HUE web server needs to be configured for secured SSL access.

Refer to the HUE Project for more details on installation and configuration: http://gethue.com/.

Knox Gateway Server

Knox Gateway is another Apache project in incubation stage that addresses the concern of secured access to the Hadoop cluster from corporate networks. Knox Gateway provides a single point-to-point of authentication and access for Apache Hadoop services in a cluster. Knox runs as cluster of servers in the DMZ zone isolating the Hadoop cluster with in the corporate network. The key feature of Knox Gateway is that it provides perimeter security for Hadoop REST APIs by limiting the network endpoints required to access a Hadoop cluster. Thus, it hides the internal Hadoop cluster topology from end users. Knox provides a single point for authentication and token verification at the perimeter of the Hadoop cluster. It enables integration with the EIM system for authentication and authorization of Hadoop services.

The following diagram shows the Knox Gateway's interaction with an end user:

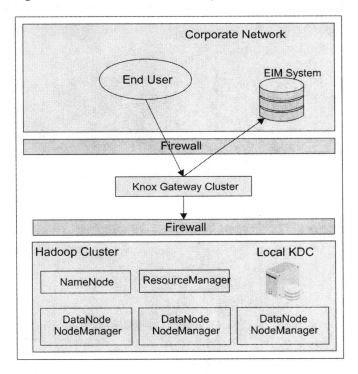

Knox is still maturing and is currently under Version 0.3. While the roadmap looks promising, it still needs to mature before it can be deployed for production usage. HUE can be configured to work with Knox Gateway instead of HttpFS and this will be more secured compared to HttpFS.

Summary

In this chapter, we looked at the various challenges for integrating a secured Hadoop cluster with Enterprise systems. One of the main concerns for organizations adopting Big Data is its security. Having the ability to manage Hadoop users' identity and authorizations centrally using existing EIM systems clears the first hurdle in the Big Data adoption journey. In this chapter, we looked at the implementation details for integrating EIM systems with the Hadoop KDC and how seamlessly Enterprise existing security process can be easily extended to Hadoop. Another big concern for organizations is usually around network security. In this chapter, we detailed out the implementation approach to enforce perimeter security around the Hadoop cluster and how to provide end users with seamless access from corporate networks to the secured Hadoop cluster using HttpFS, HUE, and Knox Gateway Server.

In the next chapter, we look at another important security concern for Big Data adoption and that is about securing sensitive data residing in the Hadoop cluster.

6
Securing Sensitive Data in Hadoop

In *Chapter 5, Integrating Hadoop with Enterprise Security Systems*, we looked at integrating a secured Hadoop cluster with an Enterprise Identity Management system and enforce user authorization within Hadoop. User privileges are managed centrally and then synchronized with the secured Hadoop cluster. This enables enterprise users to access secured Hadoop services seamlessly. As an organization matures with their Big Data implementations, there is an increasing need to move sensitive information into the Hadoop ecosystem to generate valuable insights. Sensitive data in the cluster needs special protection and should be secured both at rest and in motion.

In this chapter, we look at how to secure sensitive data within a Hadoop ecosystem.

These are the topics we'll be covering in this chapter:

- Securing sensitive data in Hadoop
- Encrypting sensitive data in Hadoop
- Implementing data encryption in Hadoop

Securing sensitive data in Hadoop

Sensitive data inside Hadoop can be classified into two high-level categories:

- Sensitive data related to customers' personal information, customers' financial information, and so on that exists in enterprise systems and that needs to be brought to Hadoop for analysis.

- The Hadoop analytical process generates sensitive insights after processing the data stored inside Hadoop. These insights are more valuable and sensitive compared to the raw source data that is used to generate them. For example, a retail e-commerce enterprise has detailed transactions of customer purchases. These transaction details might not be very sensitive. This data is brought to Hadoop for generating various insights. Using the customer historical purchases and correlating the same with customer's household purchases, insights related to customer purchase patterns, behavior patterns, customer sentiment, and customer life events could be inferred. This information is highly sensitive compared to each of the individual transactions. These insights if not secured properly could lead to significant losses for an enterprise.

Due to the schema-less, distributed nature of Hadoop, securing insights generated from Hadoop is one of the most challenging tasks in a production scenario. The Hadoop ecosystem currently lacks a robust metadata management solution to secure these insights.

The key requirements for securing this sensitive data are:

- The insights generated should be classified and encrypted so that only authorized users can access the insights.

- Only a limited set of users who really need to act on sensitive data should have access to these data sets. Data access should be restricted for any non-business user (IT user) for these sensitive data sets.

- The intermediate data that is created during the insights generation process should be secured and removed as soon as it is not required.

- Need to track which user has downloaded the sensitive insights and control the life cycle of such downloaded insights. This is required to ensure compliance.

- Access to these sensitive data sets and any other local copy of the insights should be removed once the user ceases to have authorization to access the data sets.

- The data that is in motion during storing and retrieving the data from Hadoop needs to be secured.

Approach for securing insights in Hadoop

To secure sensitive data sets in Hadoop, there should be proper security measures to secure these data sets while they are residing in Hadoop or while they are transferred across the network. To protect the data in motion, it is required to understand the underlying protocol that is used when data is transferred over the network in Hadoop. A Hadoop client connects to NameNode using the Hadoop RPC protocol over TCP, while the Hadoop client transfers the data to DataNode using the HTTP protocol over TCP.

Securing data in motion

Data enters the Hadoop ecosystem through the Hadoop client, Sqoop, or Flume. This data needs to be protected during the transfer to the Hadoop system. The SASL authentication framework is used for encrypting the data in motion.

SASL is the authentication framework that adds authentication support for connection-based protocols. SASL security guarantees that data exchanged between the client and servers is encrypted and is not readable by a "man in the middle". SASL supports multiple authentication mechanisms, for example, DIGEST-MD5, CRAM-MD5, and so on. Typically, a SASL negotiation works as follows:

1. The client requests authentication by connecting to the server.
2. The server responds with a list of supported authentication mechanisms.
3. The client chooses one of the authentication mechanisms (for example DIGEST-MD5).
4. The server then starts exchanging authentication messages with the client, until the authentication succeeds or fails.
5. Once the authentication succeeds, the client and server shares the session secrets, which are used to encrypt the transmitted data.
6. SSL uses the public key cryptography for authentication. So to verify the authenticity of the request between the client and server, both needs to have a shared secret.

SSL provides secured communication between the client and server. SSL enables encryption of the message that is exchanged once the trust between the client and server is established. This ensures that the communication using SSL is secured.

The Hadoop client uses Hadoop RPC to communicate with the Hadoop NameNode (refer to the following figure). The Hadoop RPC mechanism supports SASL security. SASL encryption can be enabled by configuring the property `hadoop.rpc.protection` to privacy in `core-site.xml`. This ensures that the communication between the Hadoop client and NameNode is secured and encrypted.

Data transfer from the Hadoop client to DataNode uses the Hadoop data transfer protocol that is built on top of TCP/IP. An SASL wrapper is required on top of the Hadoop data transfer protocol to ensure secured data transfer between the Hadoop client and DataNode. This wrapper is enabled by setting the property `dfs.encrypt.data.transfer` to `true` in `hdfs-site.xml`. Once the SASL wrapper is enabled, NameNode generates a data encryption key that is used by the Hadoop client as the credentials for the MD5-DIGEST SASL authentication mechanism. Since DataNode and NameNode share the secret key, this key can be used to verify the authenticity of the request.

Sqoop, by default, doesn't provide any security for data in motion. However, Sqoop uses JDBC within the MapReduce program to move data from RDBMS to Hadoop. The JDBC communication can be secured using the SASL with JDBC.

Flume is another ecosystem component that is used to ingest data into Hadoop. Flume uses the AVRO-RPC listen source to move data into Hadoop. Since Version 1.4, Flume AVRO-RPC supports secured SSL transport.

The following properties need to be set to ensure that SSL support for AVO-RPC is enabled.

Property	Description
Ssl	The SSL flag should be set to `true`. The default value is `false`.
Keystore	This specifies the path to the Java keystore file.
Keystore-password	This specifies the password for the Java keystore.
Keystore-type	This specifies the type of the Java keystore. This can be JKS or PKCS12. By default, it is JKS.

Securing data at rest

Hadoop stores data by splitting large files into blocks. These blocks are stored in the local filesystem of DataNode. The individual blocks can be assembled back to retrieve the entire file. Once the login credentials for the user (root or HDFS) who has access to the data node is compromised, the blocks stored in the local filesystem can be accessed. Thus, the sensitive data sets can be compromised by just breaking the security credentials of the root or HDFS user. One solution to this problem is to encrypt the file that is stored in Hadoop so that even if the login credential is compromised, the data stored inside the sensitive data sets can't be accessed. There are two ways for encrypting the data sets in Hadoop.

First, when we store the file in Hadoop, the entire file can be encrypted first and then stored in Hadoop. In this approach, the data blocks in each DataNode can't be decrypted unless we assemble all the blocks back and create the encrypted file. This approach is not suitable if the encrypted file needs to be accessed in MapReduce programs. MapReduce programs read blocks of data, and hence won't be able to decrypt the file. Then, the only option is to process the file in its entirety in JobTracker. This is very inefficient and is not a scalable solution.

The second option is to apply the encryption on the blocks of data once it is loaded into Hadoop. This ensures that MapReduce can process each block independently, and the decryption logic is applied during the map phase for a MapReduce job. The decryption key should be made available to the MapReduce job to decrypt the file. This is provided to the MapReduce program through the job configuration. The solution is scalable and efficient. This approach is shown in the following figure:

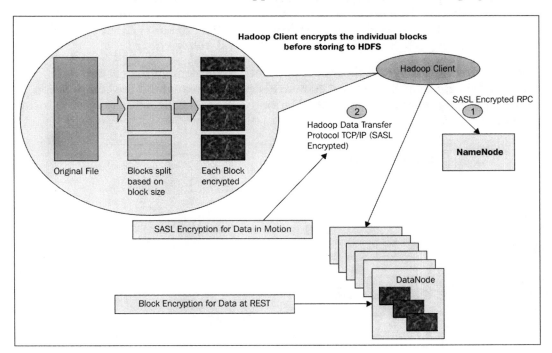

To support block-level encryption in Hadoop, the client should encrypt each individual blocks before it is transferred to DataNode for storing. Similarly, when the file has to be reconstructed, the client will read each individual blocks and then apply the decryption logic in the client side. This approach enables the client to manage the encryption credentials and not store them in the Hadoop cluster.

Currently, block-level encryption is not supported by default in Hadoop. There are open source projects such as Project Rhino (`https://github.com/intel-hadoop/project-rhino/`) that aims to bring an end-to-end encryption framework into Hadoop. The work is still in progress (`https://issues.apache.org/jira/browse/HADOOP-9331`) and till then if we want to implement the block-level compression, we need to write custom code to support this block-level encryption.

Implementing data encryption in Hadoop

Encryption is one of the key techniques used to secure sensitive data in Hadoop. Support for data encryption is not directly available in Hadoop; however, we can leverage the compression file handling capability to build support for encryption. We create a custom compression codec that supports encryption. So whenever we need to encrypt the data, we need to set the compression codec to this custom compression codec. This is the same technique used by Project Rhino. A sample compression codec is available at the following location: `https://github.com/delipark/encrypted-hdfs/` by *Seonyoung Park* and *Youngseok Lee*.

The following flow diagram shows the approach to implement the custom data encryption in Hadoop. To support custom encryption, we extend the compression codec class that is available within the Hadoop API and implement encryption inside this class.

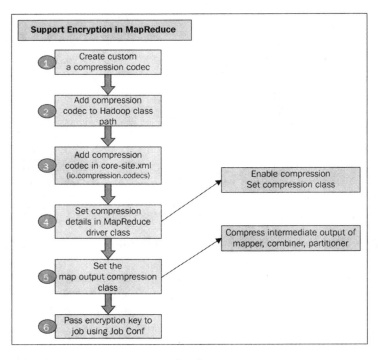

The following are the configuration files that need to be configured to support encryption using the preceding approach:

Conf file	Property	Description
core-site.xml	io.compression.codecs	Sets the class name of the custom compression codec that is implemented to support encryption.
mapred-site.xml	mapreduce.map.output.compress	Sets to true to compress the outputs of the maps before sent across the network.
mapred-site.xml	mapreduce.map.output.compress.codec	Sets this to the class name of the custom compression codec that implements encryption.
mapred-site.xml	mapreduce.output.fileoutputformat.compress	Sets to true to enforce compression of the output files created.
mapred-site.xml	mapreduce.output.fileoutputformat.compress.codec	Sets this to the class name of the custom compression codec that implements encryption.
mapred-site.xml	mapreduce.output.fileoutputformat.compress.type	Sets the compression type to BLOCK or RECORD based on the encryption algorithm support.

One important consideration in implementing encryption in Hadoop is to ensure that encryption is done at block-level, so that MapReduce can be executed efficiently and the performance degradation due to encryption is not significant. AVRO and Sequence File are two Hadoop file formats that support splits and compression formats. To support encryption in the AVRO and Sequence File formats, we need to define custom compression codecs that will implement the encryption as part of the compression process and enable AVRO and Sequence File to use this compression codec.

During the MapReduce processing, the mapper is set to read encrypted data by configuring the input compression codec and enabling compression on the input format. The key for decryption is passed to the mapper as part of the job configurations or by directly reading from the keystore. Encrypted data is read, and processed intermediate results are stored locally on the TaskTracker nodes. These intermediate results should be encrypted and for this, we can set the map output compression class to the custom compression code class. These intermediate results are then read by the reducers to produce the final result. The final result can be encrypted by setting the output compression class to the custom compression codec.

The data from the Hadoop ecosystem is consumed by exporting the data to RDBMS systems or consuming it from the NoSQL solution such as HBase, which is housed inside Hadoop.

When the data is exported from the Hadoop ecosystem to RDBMS, the export program has to decrypt the data and secure it during transit using some of the data in motion encryption techniques. Similarly, when the data is exposed out of HBase, the data is decrypted to render to the required user. The data is decrypted using the secured key provided by the end user who is consuming the data. One of the key requirements within the enterprise is to support user-classification-level security. Sensitive data within the enterprise is classified into multiple security levels. Users are then selectively authorized for these security levels and provided access to these classified data based on their roles and business functions.

To implement a user-classification-based security in Hadoop, we can extend the data encryption technique mentioned earlier. Here is the approach to implement such a user-classification-based security in a Hadoop ecosystem:

1. Each security classification level is defined with a unique encryption key and this encryption key is stored in the credential vault. Only users who are authorized for the corresponding security classification level can request for the encryption key.

2. The sensitive data is encrypted using this encryption key based on the security classification level of the data.

3. When a user runs a MapReduce job that accesses a classified dataset, the encryption key corresponding to that security classification level is fetched from the credential vault and passed to the MapReduce job through the job configuration. The credential vault will return the encryption keys only if the user is authorized for the corresponding security classification level.

This entire process of identifying the dataset classification level and fetching the corresponding encryption key for the user from the credential vault is transparently implemented in the MapReduce driver program. This entire process can be transparently implemented without any change from the end user.

Summary

In this chapter, we looked at how to secure sensitive data in the Hadoop cluster. We looked at the approaches for encryption of data in motion while block-level encryption for data is at rest. We also looked at the MapReduce processing and ways to enforce data encryption on the input side, intermediate data, and the final results created by the MapReduce program. Encryption causes performance degradation and this has to be carefully evaluated so that only sensitive data is encrypted and secured.

In the next chapter, we will look at how to identify security incidents and events in a secured Hadoop cluster. And we will also look at how to implement auditing and logging of user activities in the Hadoop cluster.

7
Security Event and Audit Logging in Hadoop

In *Chapter 6, Securing Sensitive Data in Hadoop*, we looked at the approach to secure sensitive data in a Hadoop cluster, and how we could implement block-level encryption to protect sensitive data. In this chapter, we look at security incidents and event monitoring that needs to be implemented in a secured Hadoop cluster. We then discussed the best practices in security procedures and policies that need to be adopted to secure the Hadoop ecosystem and how some of these policies can be configured as rules in the security event and audit logging system.

A Hadoop cluster in production hosts sensitive customer information. Security of data assets is of prime importance for organizations to have a successful big data journey. While we focus on ensuring that the Hadoop cluster is secured through various measures such as enforcing perimeter security, Kerberos authentication, and authorization, there is always a possibility of security breaches by unauthorized access or inappropriate access by privileged users. So to meet the security compliance requirements, we need to audit the entire Hadoop ecosystem on a periodic basis and deploy a system that generates automated alerts by security incident and log monitoring.

In this chapter, we look at how to implement the security incident and event monitoring approach and the procedures to set up the required audit logs in Hadoop that are required for security compliance.

These are the topics we'll be covering in this chapter:

- Security Incident and Event Monitoring in a Hadoop cluster
- An overview of the Security Incident and Event Monitoring system
- Setting up audit logging in a secured Hadoop cluster

Security Incident and Event Monitoring in a Hadoop Cluster

A Security Incident and Event Monitoring (SIEM) system is responsible for collecting, monitoring, analyzing, and generating various security alerts for any suspicious activity in the cluster. SIEM systems usually collect the various system logs, network logs, and application logs to identify these security incidents and events. Hadoop itself can be used to perform the analysis and correlation of these security events in a batch mode.

The first step in any SIEM system is to collect the various system logs and identify corresponding events. The following are the events that need to be monitored in a Hadoop cluster to detect any security incidents:

- **User login and authorization events**: User login events in a secured Hadoop cluster are generated when the end users or service principals authenticate themselves within the KDC or EIM system. `krb5kdc.log` for the KDC in the local Hadoop realm will contain the service login events. The central EIM system (Active Directory or similar) will log the user authentication events. Any user request for the service tickets for the Hadoop daemons will also be logged. This will help in identifying details of the users who has requested for access to the various Hadoop services.

- **HDFS file operation errors**: Whenever a user accesses HDFS, the file permissions for the users are verified by NameNode before providing the access to the blocks for the files. In case of insufficient privileges the **org. apache.hadoop.security.AccessControlException: Permission denied** event is generated Hadoop logfiles. Any access privilege issue by Hive or Pig jobs also will generate the same error. These exceptions will be logged in to the Hadoop daemon logs in the Hadoop log directory. These exceptions should be monitored to identify potential security incidents. To ensure that file permission checks are enforced by NameNode, we need to set the property `dfs.permissions.enabled` to `true` in `hdfs-site.xml`.

- **Hadoop RPC authorization errors**: Hadoop provides the ability to control the groups/users that are authorized to use a particular Hadoop service. This authorization is enabled by setting the property `hadoop.security. authorization` to `true` in `core-site.xml`. The user/groups access details can be configured in `hadoop-policy.xml` in the `conf` folder. If there is any unauthorized access request made to the Hadoop daemons, `org.apache. hadoop.security.authorize.AuthorizationException` is logged in to the Hadoop security logfile. Monitoring these exceptions can help identify unauthorized access.

- **Hadoop RPC authentication errors**: Hadoop RPC uses Java SASL APIs for authentication. Quality of Protection (QoP) during authentication can be set for this interaction. This ensures that the client is able to securely connect with the Hadoop services and any authentication failures due to man-in-the-middle attacks can be recorded. Hadoop provides the configuration `hadoop.rpc.protection` in `core-site.xml`, which can be configured to enable authentication, integrity, and confidentiality between the client and RPC daemons. Any errors resulting from the RPC authentication are logged in the security logfile of Hadoop.

- **HDFS-sensitive file download operations**: Hadoop has the ability to log every filesystem operation to the HDFS audit logfile. This audit file can be used to identify which user has accessed the sensitive file and downloaded these files. It is important to keep an audit trail of the sensitive file access by authorized users as well. The audit log provides the ability to track sensitive file access and downloads from the Hadoop cluster. This access to sensitive files can be captured in the SIEM system and rules configured to detect any suspicious activities. These can be configured as security alerts in the SIEM system.

- **MapReduce job events**: Hadoop provides the ability to log all MapReduce job submission and execution related events in the audit log. The job submission, initialization, views, and modifications are logged in the audit logfiles. This audit logfile can be used to identify which user is accessing or running MapReduce jobs on the cluster and if there are any authentication and authorization errors, they are logged. The MapReduce job errors can be correlated with the HDFS filesystem access exceptions in the SIEM tool to detect any suspicious activities.

- **User access through Oozie, HUE, and WebHDFS**: Each user accesses Oozie and workflow submission is logged in to the Oozie audit logs. All user interactions with Oozie are logged in to the audit log. This enables you to track the details of the user that has executed a particular workflow.

  HUE provides the user interface for Hadoop. The user logs in to HUE for performing the various operations in Hadoop. Each of these interactions are logged by HUE in the HUE logs. The exception from the HUE logs can be monitored in the SIEM tool.

  Users can directly access Hadoop through the WebHDFS REST API or indirectly through HUE and Oozie. WebHDFS access logs are tracked by NameNode audit logs. Any exception in the NameNode audit logs is tracked in the SIEM tool.

- **Exception events**: Apart from the security events generated by user authentications and authorizations, it is useful to log any exceptions in the Hadoop cluster. These exceptions provide hints to potential vulnerabilities in the system and can be looked at in detail to identify potential security incidents. The SIEM tool can be used to correlate these exceptions.

The Security Incident and Event Monitoring (SIEM) system

A typical Security Incident and Event Monitoring system consists of three main components:

- **Log and event collecting agents**: These agents are installed in each of the nodes in the cluster, which needs to collect the event and audit logs. Typically, they are configured to ingest the Hadoop security audit logs and event logs and collect the required elements that are published to the Event Monitoring Server.

- **Event Monitoring Server**: These are central servers that receive the log and audit events published by collecting agents. They usually have certain listener ports which are open to listen to events published by the collecting agents. They continuously run the policy and rule evaluation on the log events that are received from the collecting agents. Based on the alert policies configured, corresponding alerts are generated, which are visible through the Event Monitoring and Audit Logging UI.

- **Event Monitoring and Audit Logging UI**: The user interface (UI) provides the ability to define the Event Monitoring policies and configure the rules for automated alerts. The UI also provides prebuilt reports that can be used to review the policy violations, access, and authorization violations along with any sensitive data access.

The block diagram of a Security Event and Audit Logging system for a secured Hadoop cluster is as follows:

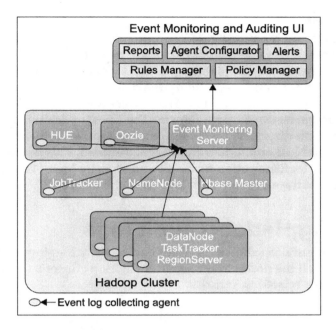

The security event logging and auditing capabilities are provided by a few products such as OSSEC. They provide the ability to configure rules that can be leveraged to set up the rule for monitoring Hadoop. For detecting security incidents and alerts from the Hadoop cluster, Hadoop audit logging needs to be enabled and configured.

OSSEC is a popular **host-based intrusion detection system (HIDS)** that is an open source project owned and sponsored by Trend Micro. OSSEC provides the capability to collect the various logs and events from the secured Hadoop cluster and process them to create alerts. The generated alerts can also be pushed to the enterprise SIEM tool for further actions. Further details on configuring OSSEC for event monitoring are provided in the following link: http://www.ossec.net/.

Hadoop provides audit logs and security logs. However, they are not enabled by default. In the next section we will see how to enable audit logging in Hadoop.

Setting up audit logging in a secured Hadoop cluster

To enable security event monitoring and auditing in Hadoop, we need to enable the logging framework to write the detailed audit trails in the logfile. Enabling detailed audit logs needs careful planning. These logs could grow very fast if there are continuous exceptions and could fill up the disk space. There should be a system monitoring this log growth and taking corrective actions such as cleaning and compressing. This can be done by configuring the Log4j.properties file in the Hadoop configuration directory. By default, the Hadoop security and audit logfile appenders are set to **Null appenders** and hence, disabled. This needs to be modified to reflect the correct logfile location for audit and security logs. We also need to enable the capture of the authentication logs from the local KDC.

Configuring Hadoop audit logs

The following configuration shows the audit and security logging configurations that need to be done on all the nodes in the secured Hadoop cluster to collect the audit and exception events related to security:

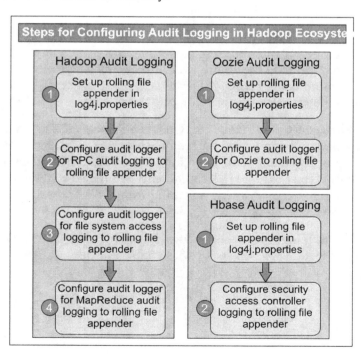

- **Common properties for rolling file appender**: These configurations need to be done in `log4j.properties` in the `/etc/hadoop/conf` directory. To enable Hadoop RPC audit logging, we need to configure the rolling file appender in `log4j.properties`. Add the following configurations that set the rolling file **appender for security logging (RFAS)**:

  ```
  hadoop.log.dir= /var/logs/auditlogs

  hadoop.security.log.file=SecurityAuth-${user.name}.audit

  log4j.appender.RFAS=org.apache.log4j.RollingFileAppender

  log4j.appender.RFAS.File=${hadoop.log.dir}/${hadoop.security.log.file}

  log4j.appender.RFAS.layout=org.apache.log4j.PatternLayout

  log4j.appender.RFAS.layout.ConversionPattern=%d{ISO8601} %p %c: %m%n

  log4j.appender.RFAS.MaxFileSize=256MB

  log4j.appender.RFAS.MaxBackupIndex=20
  ```

- **Hadoop RPC event logging**: To enable Hadoop RPC audit logging, we need to add the following logger in `log4j.properties`:

  ```
  log4j.logger.SecurityLogger=INFO, RFAS
  ```

- **Hadoop File System access audit logging**: To enable the HDFS file access audit information, we need to add the following logger:

  ```
  log4j.logger.org.apache.hadoop.hdfs.server.namenode.FSNamesystem.audit = INFO, RFAS
  ```

- **Hadoop MapReduce audit logging**: To enable the MapReduce job-submission-related audit information, we need to add the following logger:

  ```
  log4j.logger.org.apache.hadoop.mapred.AuditLogger = INFO, RFAS
  ```

- **Oozie audit logging**: To enable Oozie-related audit information in the Oozie logs, we need to configure the following logger in `log4j.properties` in the `/etc/oozie/conf` directory and also add the common properties for the rolling file appender described earlier:

  ```
  log4j.logger.oozieaudit = INFO, RFAS
  ```

- **HBase audit logging**: To enable HBase user-level access-related audit information in the Oozie logs, we need to configure the following logger in `log4j.properties` in the `/etc/hbase/conf` directory along with common properties for the rolling file appender described earlier:

  ```
  log4j.logger.SecurityLogger.org.apache.hadoop.hbase.security.access.AccessController= INFO, RFAS
  ```

- **HUE audit logging**: HUE provides `access.log`, which has all user-access-related audit information in the location `/var/log/hue` or the logs directory inside the installation folder.

- **KDC audit logging**: In a secured Hadoop cluster, the Hadoop services will authenticate with the local KDC using the service principal, and also, all the users will contact the local KDC to fetch the service tickets for accessing the Hadoop services. These audit events can be captured and logged in to a specific directory. To configure the kadmind and krb5kdc processes to log the access logs in the specified directory, we need to update the `kdc.conf` logging section. For example, add the following entry in the `kdc.conf` logging section:

```
[logging]
            kdc = FILE:/var/log/kdc-audit.log
    admin_server = FILE:/var/log/kadmin.log
```

Once the setup of the audit logging is completed in Hadoop, HBase, Oozie, HUE, and local KDC, the audit logs have to be configured in the collection agent to fetch the logs and process them. These configurations are specific to the SIEM tool that is deployed and the corresponding documentation has to be referred to configure it. The collection agent parses the logfile and extracts the required fields. Then, it publishes the events to the monitoring server. The monitoring server executes the rules and policies configured on these events and generates the alerts and reports.

Summary

In this chapter we looked at the general approach for identifying security incidents and events in a secured Hadoop cluster. The SIEM systems consists of a collection agent that gathers the events from the cluster and publishes them to the monitoring server. The monitoring server is configured with rules and policies that are applied on the collected events to generate security alerts and reports. We also looked at how we configure the audit and security logs for the various components in a secured Hadoop cluster.

Solutions Available for Securing Hadoop

This section will focus on providing an overview of the various commercial and open source technologies that are available to address the various security aspects, and how they fit into the reference architecture of securing enterprise Big Data assets.

Hadoop distribution with enhanced security support

Intel Distribution of Apache Hadoop software provides some enhanced security features in a Hadoop distribution. Some of the key features for Intel's distribution are:

- It provides an integrated data encryption feature for sensitive data. The encryption is based on OpenSSL 1.0.1.C, which is optimized for Intel AES-NI.

- Apart from encryption, Intel's distribution supports out of the box compression and encryption capabilities.

- Sensitive data is never exposed either in motion or at rest. Thus, it is used to ingest encrypted data into the Hadoop ecosystem and process the encrypted data. Encryption keys are integrated using the Java keystore functionality.

- Intel's Manager for Apache Hadoop Software provides deployment, management, monitoring, alerting, and security features.

- It provides a feature for managing user access to data and services using Kerberos by creating access control lists (ACLs) and limiting user access to data sets and services.

- Deployment and setup of the secure Hadoop cluster is automated and integrated with key management systems.

[More details on Intel's Hadoop Distribution are available at https://hadoop.intel.com.]

Automation of a secured Hadoop cluster deployment

Let us have a look at some of the most important tools.

Cloudera Manager

Cloudera Manager is another of the most popular Hadoop Management and Deployment Tool. Some of the key features of Cloudera Manager with respect to securing a Hadoop Cluster are:

- Cloudera Manager automates the entire Hadoop cluster setup and enables an automated setup of a secure Hadoop cluster with Kerberos. Cloudera Manager automatically sets up the Keytab file in all the slave nodes, and updates the Hadoop configuration with the required Keytab locations and service principal details. Cloudera Manager updates the configuration files (`core-site.xml`, `hdfs-site.xml`, `mapred-site.xml`, `oozie-site.xml`, `hue.ini`, and `taskcontroller.cfg`) without any manual intervention.

- It supports the deployment of a role-based administration, where there are read-only administrators who monitor the cluster while others can change the deployments.

- It enables administrators to configure alerts specific to user activity and access. This can be leveraged to security incidents and event monitoring.

- Cloudera can send events to enterprise SIEM tools about security incidents in Hadoop using SNMP.

- It can integrate user credentials using LDAP with Active Directory.

[More details on Cloudera Manager are available at the following URL: http://www.cloudera.com/content/cloudera/en/products/cloudera-manager.html.]

Zettaset

Zettaset (`http://www.zettaset.com/`) provides a product Zettaset Orchestrator that provides seamless secured Hadoop deployment and management. Zettaset doesn't provide any Hadoop distribution, but works with all distributions such as Cloudera, Hortonworks, and Apache Hadoop. Some of the key features of the Zettaset Orchestrator are:

- It provides an automated deployment of a secured Hadoop cluster
- It hardens the entire Hadoop deployment from an enterprise perspective to address policy, compliance, access control, and risk management within the Hadoop cluster environment
- It integrates seamlessly with an existing enterprise security policy framework using LDAP and Active Directory (AD)
- It provides centralized configuration management, logging, and auditing
- It provides **role-based access controls** (**RBACs**) and enables Kerberos to be seamlessly integrated with the rest of the ecosystem

All other platform management tools such as Ambari and Greenplum Hadoop Deployment Manager need manual setup for establishing a secured Hadoop cluster. The Keytab files, service principals, and the configuration files have to be manually deployed on all nodes.

Different Hadoop data encryption options

Let us have a look at the various options available.

Dataguise for Hadoop

Dataguise (**DG**) for Hadoop provides a symmetric-key-based encryption of the data. One of the key features of Dataguise is to identify and encrypt sensitive data. It supports encryption and masking techniques for sensitive data protection. It enables encryption of data with Hadoop API, Sqoop, and Flume. Thus, it can be used to encrypt data moving in and out of the Hadoop ecosystem. Administrators can schedule the data scan within the Hadoop ecosystem at regular intervals, and detect sensitive data and encrypt or mask it. More details on Dataguise are available at `http://dataguise.com/products/dghadoop.html`.

Gazzang zNcrypt

Gazzang zNcrypt provides a transparent block level encryption and provides the ability to manage the keys used for encryption. zNcrypt acts like a virtual filesystem that intercepts any application layer request to access the files. It encrypts the block as it is written to the disk. zNcrypt leverages the Intel AES-NI hardware encryption acceleration for maximum performance in the cryptographic process. It also provides role-based access control and policy-based management of the encryption keys. This can be used to implement multiple classification level security in a secured Hadoop cluster.

eCryptfs for Hadoop

eCryptfs is a cryptographic stacked Linux filesystem. eCryptfs stores cryptographic metadata in the header of each file written. When the encrypted files are copied between hosts, the file will be decrypted with the proper key in the Linux kernel key ring. We can set up a secured Hadoop cluster with eCryptfs on each node. This ensures that data is transparently shared between nodes, and that all the data is encrypted before being written to the disk.

More information on eCryptfs is available in the following link:
`https://launchpad.net/ecryptfs`.

Securing the Hadoop ecosystem with Project Rhino

Project Rhino aimed to provide an integrated end-to-end data security view of the Hadoop ecosystem.

It provides the following key features:

- Hadoop crypto codec framework and crypto codec implementation to provide block-level encryption support for data stored in Hadoop
- Key distribution and management support so that MapReduce can decrypt the block and execute the program as required
- Enhancing the security features of HBase by introducing cell-level authentication for HBase, and providing transparent encryption for HBase tables stored in Hadoop
- Standardized audit logging framework and log formats for easy audit trail analysis

More details on project Rhino are available at `https://github.com/intel-hadoop/project-rhino/`.

Mapping of security technologies with the reference architecture

We looked at the various commercial and open source tools that enable securing the Big Data platform. This section provides the mapping of these various technologies and how they fit into the overall reference architecture.

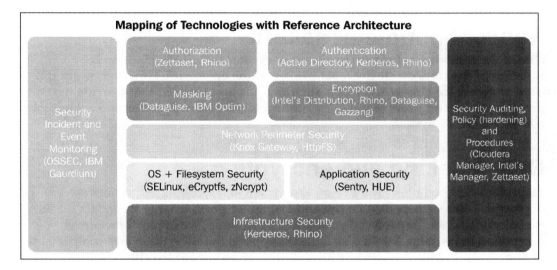

Infrastructure security

Physical security needs to be enforced manually. However, unauthorized access to a distributed cluster is avoided by deploying Kerberos security in the cluster. Kerberos ensures that the services and users confirm their identity with the KDC before they are provided access to the infrastructure services. Project Rhino aims to extend this further by providing the token-based authentication framework.

OS and filesystem security

Filesystem security is enforced by providing a secured virtualization layer on the existing OS filesystem using the file encryption technique. Files written to the disk are encrypted and while files read from the file are decrypted on-the-fly. These features are provided by eCryptfs and zNcrypt tools. SELinux also provides significant protection by hardening the OS.

Application security

Tools such as Sentry and HUE provide a platform for secured access to Hadoop. They integrate with LDAP to provide seamless enterprise integration.

Network perimeter security

One of the common techniques to ensure perimeter security in Hadoop is by isolation of the Hadoop cluster from the rest of the enterprise. However, users still need to access the cluster with tools such as Knox and HttpFS , that provide the proxy layer for end users to remotely connect to the Hadoop cluster and submit jobs and access the filesystem.

Data masking and encryption

To protect data in motion and at rest, encryption and masking techniques are deployed. Tools such as IBM Optim and Dataguise provide large scale data masking for enterprise data. To protect data in REST in Hadoop, we deploy block-level encryption in Hadoop. Intel's distribution supports the encryption and compression of files. Project Rhino enables block-level encryption similar to Dataguise and Gazzang.

Authentication and authorization

While authentication and authorization has matured significantly, tools such as Zettaset Orchestrator and Project Rhino enable integration with the enterprise system for authentication and authorization.

Audit logging, security policies, and procedures

Common Security Audit logging for user access to Hadoop Cluster is enabled by tools such as Cloudera Manager. Cloudera Manager also has the ability to generate alerts and events based on the configured organizational policies. Similarly, Intel's manager and Zettaset Orchestrator also provide the security policies enforcement in the cluster as per organizational policies.

Security Incident and Event Monitoring

Detecting security incident and monitoring events in a Big Data platform is essential. Open source tools such as OSSEC and IBM Gaudium enable a secured Hadoop cluster to detect security incidents and provide easy integration with enterprise SIEM tools.

Index

Thank you for buying
Securing Hadoop

About Packt Publishing

Packt, pronounced 'packed', published its first book "*Mastering phpMyAdmin for Effective MySQL Management*" in April 2004 and subsequently continued to specialize in publishing highly focused books on specific technologies and solutions.

Our books and publications share the experiences of your fellow IT professionals in adapting and customizing today's systems, applications, and frameworks. Our solution based books give you the knowledge and power to customize the software and technologies you're using to get the job done. Packt books are more specific and less general than the IT books you have seen in the past. Our unique business model allows us to bring you more focused information, giving you more of what you need to know, and less of what you don't.

Packt is a modern, yet unique publishing company, which focuses on producing quality, cutting-edge books for communities of developers, administrators, and newbies alike. For more information, please visit our website: www.packtpub.com.

About Packt Open Source

In 2010, Packt launched two new brands, Packt Open Source and Packt Enterprise, in order to continue its focus on specialization. This book is part of the Packt Open Source brand, home to books published on software built around Open Source licences, and offering information to anybody from advanced developers to budding web designers. The Open Source brand also runs Packt's Open Source Royalty Scheme, by which Packt gives a royalty to each Open Source project about whose software a book is sold.

Writing for Packt

We welcome all inquiries from people who are interested in authoring. Book proposals should be sent to author@packtpub.com. If your book idea is still at an early stage and you would like to discuss it first before writing a formal book proposal, contact us; one of our commissioning editors will get in touch with you.

We're not just looking for published authors; if you have strong technical skills but no writing experience, our experienced editors can help you develop a writing career, or simply get some additional reward for your expertise.

Hadoop Beginner's Guide

ISBN: 978-1-84951-730-0   Paperback: 398 pages

Learn how to crunch big data to extract meaning from the data avalanche

1. Learn tools and techniques that let you approach Big Data with relish and not fear

2. Shows how to build a complete infrastructure to handle your needs as your data grows

3. Hands-on examples in each chapter give the big picture while also giving direct experience

Scaling Big Data with Hadoop and Solr

ISBN: 978-1-78328-137-4   Paperback: 144 pages

Learn exciting new ways to build effi cient, high performance enterprise search repositories for Big Data using Hadoop and Solr

1. Understand the different approaches of making Solr work on Big Data as well as the benefits and drawbacks

2. Learn from interesting, real-life use cases for Big Data search along with sample code

3. Work with the Distributed Enterprise Search without prior knowledge of Hadoop and Solr

Please check **www.PacktPub.com** for information on our titles

Hadoop MapReduce Cookbook

ISBN: 978-1-84951-728-7   Paperback: 300 pages

Recipes for analyzing large and complex datasets with Hadoop MapReduce

1. Learn to process large and complex data sets, starting simply, then diving in deep

2. Solve complex big data problems such as classifications, finding relationships, online marketing and recommendations

3. More than 50 Hadoop MapReduce recipes, presented in a simple and straightforward manner, with step-by-step instructions and real world examples

Hadoop Real-World Solutions Cookbook

ISBN: 978-1-84951-912-0   Paperback: 316 pages

Realistic, simple code examples to solve problems at scale with Hadoop and related technologies

1. Solutions to common problems when working in the Hadoop environment

2. Recipes for (un)loading data, analytics, and troubleshooting

3. In depth code examples demonstrating various analytic models, analytic solutions, and common best practices

Please check **www.PacktPub.com** for information on our titles

CPSIA information can be obtained at www.ICGtesting.com
Printed in the USA
BVOW05s0741310114

343489BV00004BA/107/P